S mac Leon Gulman
ANTS 1962

EARLY
CHRISTIAN
ORIGINS

HAROLD R. WILLOUGHBY

EARLY CHRISTIAN ORIGINS

Studies in honor of
Harold R. Willoughby
Edited by
Allen Wikgren

QUADRANGLE BOOKS
CHICAGO 1961

© 1961 by Quadrangle Books, Inc.

Library of Congress Catalog Card Number 61-7933

Designed by Greer Allen

First published 1961 by
QUADRANGLE BOOKS, INC.
119 West Lake Street, Chicago 1, Illinois

PRINTED IN THE U.S.A.

Dedicated by Former Colleagues and Students

to HAROLD R. WILLOUGHBY

Professor Emeritus of Early Christian Origins
of The University of Chicago
in his Seventieth Year

PREFACE

The whole matter of Christian origins has become in recent years the subject of much discussion among scholars, and also of wide concern among many laymen. A great amount of this interest has been stimulated by the discoveries of the Qumran scrolls, but other important data have also contributed. The Gnostic library found in Egypt has just begun to be available. Much significant archeological discovery continues at the present time. Some of the earliest documents of the Greek New Testament are just coming to light, notably those of the Bodmer Library. Literary interpretation has again involved problems of historical reconstruction, as in the so-called "demythologizing" controversies, which continue strong today. These include the question of the contemporary relevance of the documents of early Christianity, an area of current concern in relation to the theological use and interpretation of the Bible and to a theological and philosophical understanding of the nature and destiny of man. The present world situation has led to renewed comparative study of Christian and other historic world religions, which have begun to grope toward some common ground in the face of dialectical materialism and growing secularism. For similar reasons integrative and ecumenical movements continue within Christendom, the basis for these always involving questions of the meaning and relevance of the "apostolic witness" reflected in the earliest documents of the Christian faith.

The present volume treats certain main topics of concern in this area from the standpoint of biblical scholarship; and these investigations illustrate the kind of study that must support any valid generalizations and conclusions about Christian beginnings. In this and other areas of scholarly inquiry Professor Willoughby himself has produced exemplary studies, and his many students inevitably have inherited something of his spirit and method.

Two members of Dr. Willoughby's last seminar of his teaching career at Chicago, Rodney Hood and Horst Moehring, deserve mention here for their enthusiastic interest in the preparation of a volume of studies such as this, and it seemed fitting that they should contribute essays of their own to the collection. I wish also to thank Dr. Hood for assistance in various ways during my absence from the country in the winter of 1960. It goes without saying that we are deeply grateful to all of the contributors, whose generous and valued cooperation has made the publication possible.

ALLEN WIKGREN

CONTENTS

I | *Rodney T. Hood*
FRANKLIN COLLEGE

THE GENEALOGIES
OF JESUS

Among the many *forms* found in the Synoptic Gospels, the analysis of which has become a popular field of study, there is one which form criticism has largely ignored. This is the genealogy, represented principally by Matt. 1:1-17 and Luke 3:23-38. The paucity of the material partly accounts for its relative neglect, although one suspects that another reason is the general viewpoint that the records of Jesus' alleged hereditary background are unedifying and unimportant. It is perhaps natural that such study should lack appeal and should be therefore passed over for more promising research into his environment. But genealogy has its environment too. This environment invites exploration, for it provides a context which may illuminate our understanding of early Christian attitudes toward Jesus.

The student who looks for evidences of the use of genealogy in the ancient world finds them everywhere—among Jews and Gentiles, gods and men, kings and priests, nobles and parvenus; within Scripture and without; in both literary and non-literary sources. A selection from this wealth of material will provide examples which will illustrate six basically representative functions of genealogy in antiquity. With such a background we shall then examine the genealogies of Matthew and Luke. These six aspects are not mutually exclusive; indeed, they blend and mingle often in exasperating fashion. Moreover, the terminology is not ancient but modern. Nevertheless, with this caveat, and with the further warning that the examples cited are not to be treated as "parallels" to the gospel pedigrees, we may consider them as categories for organizing the material.

1. IDENTIFICATION.—The most obvious function of the genealogy

of an individual is to indicate simply who he is. As in the Scandinavian and other countries to this day, an incipient genealogy could serve as a person's name. Joshua, Son of Nun, Isaiah, son of Amoz, and Simon, son of Jonah are familiar Biblical examples. Among Greeks it was common for one of an ancient family to have three names, his own, his patronymic, and the name of his family, such as Μιλτιάδης Κίμωνος Δαιάδης. When a son is born, until he acquires individuality he is of importance chiefly by virtue of relationship to his father. Occasionally the son continues to be known in this way, as the two disciples of Jesus who are sometimes called merely "the sons of Zebedee," or the blind beggar who is known only as "the son of Timaeus." [1]

The addition of a patronymic to a personal name served to limit the range of application of the name to a small number of individuals, or to just one, in a restricted context. Where more precise identification was necessary, the grandfather's name could be added. In legal documents from Egypt during the Ptolemaic and Roman periods an even fuller genealogical identification is common. In an apprenticeship contract from Oxyrhynchus (A.D. 66) for one Thounis, we are told the names of his father and mother, his paternal grandfather and grandmother, his paternal great-grandfather, and the fathers of his mother and grandmother. [2] Marriage contracts, wills, and other documents frequently provide material for a pedigree of several generations.

Another aspect of identification in genealogy occurs where a longer pedigree is given in order to place an individual in his proper setting within a larger kinship group. Thus we may have A designated not simply as son of B but as descendant of C, with the intermediate links supplied. So in Zeph. 1:1 we have Zephaniah further identified as a great-great-grandson of Hezekiah, doubtless intended as King Hezekiah of Judah. A rather unusual pedigree in the book of Judith presents us with Judith's line of descent for sixteen generations, terminating in "Salasadai son of Israel." [3] Here, of course, as often elsewhere, the phrase *son of* must mean *descendant of* and represents omitted generations.

2. ORGANIZATION.—An ancient use of genealogy is to indicate a relationship (in the most general sense) between individuals in terms of relationship by blood. As such, genealogy becomes a principle of organization, a vehicle for presenting myths and

---

[1] Matt. 20:20; Mark 10:6.
[2] George Milligan, *Selections from the Greek Papyri* (Cambridge, 1912), No. 20.
[3] Jth. 8:1.

legends, a method of writing history, not to say a substitute for history. Hesiod's *Theogony* represents an early Greek effort to deal with the primeval period by means of pedigrees which show relationships among the gods and between gods and men. Acusilaus of Argos, Hecataeus of Miletus and Hellanicus of Mytilene are other early writers of genealogical history. In Genesis the genealogies of Cain's descendants (4:17-22) and of the patriarchal ancestors of Israel are good examples of this type, which are later modified and extended in Chronicles.[4] The terms in such a genealogy may be only quasi-personal, actually referring to peoples and their presumed connections. Thus we have in the Greek genealogies a primitive ethnological classification of various Hellenic peoples, with *Dorus, Aeolus, Ion,* and *Achaeus* as sons and grandsons of Hellen.[5] Similarly, in Genesis we find Mizraim and Canaan listed among the sons of Ham and Moab given as a son of Lot and great-nephew of Abraham.[6]

The tendency toward systematization makes for invented connections whereby unrelated figures become joined in a pedigree. The evidence for such connections may be merely traditions of successive occupancy of the same region or contact of some other sort. A related tendency is seen in the tradition incorporated in the New Testament whereby John the Baptist becomes a second (or more distant) cousin to Jesus. Later developments of this sort produced relationships between Jesus and certain of his disciples.

The functions of organization and identification merge in the development of interest in the names of a man's ancestors or near relations for their own sake. Usually such antiquarian interest arises long after the materials for satisfying it are lost. An outstanding example is Jubilees, which attempts to satisfy later curiosity as to the wives of the patriarchs as well as their parents and children. A similar interest is shown in the attention given to the parentage and relatives of Mary in the New Testament apocrypha.

3. MAGNIFICATION.—In the New Testament period, as often before and since, genealogy was used as a support for individual and family pride. The longer one's pedigree and the more illustrious the names in it, the better. The writer of the *Rhetoric to*

---

[4] Philo calls Moses a genealogist, Abraham 31. The book of Chronicles is called the "book of genealogies" in rabbinic sources. Polybius, in discussing methods of writing history, mentions a genealogical method which he prefers not to use, although he knows that it interests many readers (ix, 1.3).

[5] Leonard Whibley, ed., *A Companion to Greek Studies* (Cambridge, 1916), p. 74.

[6] Gen. 10:7, 19:6.

Alexander (allegedly by Aristotle but probably composed a century after him) discusses genealogy and its use in orations. Observing that pedigree forms the basis of credit or discredit in men as well as animals, he says that in giving the eulogy of an individual one should always give his lineage—that is, provided his ancestors are distinguished men. For, he says, "It is clear that those descended from good backgrounds resemble their ancestors." If only the recent ancestors have been prominent, one must contrive to pass over the earlier ones. If none of them is outstanding, it is best to omit reference to them entirely and rather to ridicule the custom of praising one's ancestors, since so often the descendants of a great man turn out badly. On the other hand, if the speaker's purpose is the denunciation of his subject, he should make advantageous use of bad ancestry.[7]

Among old Roman families it was customary to portray the ancestry in the home by means of a *stemma*. The ancestors were represented by wax masks mounted in cabinets on the wall and connected by lines to show the relationships. At the death of a member of the family, retainers wore these masks while marching in the funeral procession. Such displays of genealogy, whatever the religious origin of these practices, served to enhance the prestige of the family of the deceased.

In his autobiography Josephus remarks that just as each nation has its own measure of nobility, "so with us descent from the priesthood is the sure proof of family distinction." His own family, he says, were not only priests but members of the first of the twenty-four *courses* of the priesthood. Not only that, his mother was of Maccabean descent. With this dazzling pedigree, which he gives in detail to the fifth generation, he feels that his would-be slanderers are effectively silenced.[8]

Because of this attitude toward genealogy, it is not surprising that many pedigrees were fabricated. By loose application of etymological guesses or on even less evidence, the derivation of a family from an ancient king or god could easily be arranged. There was no College of Heralds to regulate the drawing up of pedigrees, and there was every opportunity for the enterprising genealogist to provide the newly rich with a distinguished lineage. Plutarch observes, in speaking of the various traditions of his time concerning the progeny of Numa Pompilius, that one group of writers was accused of currying favor with certain noble Roman families by

[7] *Rhetoric to Alexander* xxxv.
[8] *Life* 1-6.

producing for them fictitious lines of descent from Numa.[9] The encyclopaedic Varro wrote in the first century B.C. a book about those families which claimed descent from Aeneas and his countrymen.[10] Galba was proud of his own ancestry. While emperor he "displayed a *stemma* in his atrium in which he traced his father's origin back to Jupiter and his mother's to Pasiphae the wife of Minos."[11] And the poet Horace mockingly derived the family of Aelius Lamia from Lamus, a cannibal king of the Laestrygonians.[12] Such satire only shows the lengths to which adulation of ancestry had gone.

4. CHARACTERIZATION. Not only did a man's genealogy indicate how great he was; more generally, it showed what sort of person he was. Thus it was used also for its descriptive value. Theophrastus, in his *Character* on "Backbiting," says that the backbiter will tell you who a person is in the way that genealogists do, namely, by telling you his background. Then after slandering the man's father and mother and after ridiculing his changes of name (which supposedly reveal his rise from the lower to the higher classes of society), he will add, "coming from such a stock, he is a wicked rascal."[13]

Julius Caesar gave an illustration of this aspect of genealogy at the funeral of his aunt Julia. In speaking of her he said, "The maternal ancestry of my aunt is traced to kings, the paternal to the immortal gods. For the *Marcii Reges* (her mother's family) are descended from Ancus Marcius; the *Julii*, to which we belong, are descended from Venus. Therefore in our family is the sanctity of kings, who have supreme power among men, and the venerability of the gods, to whose power kings themselves are subject."[14] We may be confident that Caesar was making a claim for himself as well as his aunt in this address. The well-known inscription of the princeling Antiochus of Commagene, erected in the late first century B. C., includes in his laudatory self-portrait a characterization by genealogy—that he was son of the Victorious King Mithridates and of Laodice the Brother-loving Goddess, the daughter of King Antiochus Epiphanes, the Mother-loving, the Victorious. No doubt functions of magnification and characterization are both present in this inscription.

[9] *Numa* 21. 2.
[10] *de familiis Troianis.*
[11] Suetonius, *Galba* 2.
[12] *Odes* iii. 17.
[13] *Characters* xxviii. 12.
[14] Suetonius, *Julius* 6.

In the New Testament, the Jews of Jesus' day are denounced as sons of their fathers who persecuted the prophets, for they persecute *the Prophet*. In spite of their claim that they would not have done so had they lived in the days of their fathers, they witness against themselves, in that they are the sons of those who murdered the prophets.[15] In this we see the descriptive meaning of the phrase *son of*, which is common in Hebrew and Aramaic where genealogical language is used for characterization. To a limited extent, this usage is also found in Latin and Greek.

5. QUALIFICATION.—In addition to indicating quality in its subject, genealogy gave him certain corresponding privileges. Either by law or by custom it entitled him to particular roles in society, civil, economic and religious. The son of a slave was automatically a slave. The son of a craftsman tended to follow in his father's footsteps. The son of a man was ordinarily an heir to his father's property. The son of a king was ordinarily an heir to the throne. Conversely, genealogy could be used to support a claim by a son to a privilege or honor.

When Herod the Great ascended the throne of Judea he took to wife (in 37 B.C.) Mariamme, the granddaughter of two Maccabean rulers and niece of a third (and the last), no doubt in the hope of strengthening his title to the kingdom by ties of blood to the former ruling family. Likewise, his record of liquidating surviving members of that family is explained by the fact that any one of them might come to be regarded by the people as their rightful king and hence Herod's rival. Similarly, throughout ancient history there are numerous examples of the overthrow of a dynasty accompanied by the death or banishment of all survivers of the deposed king. One thus inherited the disgrace of a father. It was a common experience that one also inherited the fruit of the sin or folly of a forebear. In spite of prophetic protest, it was a proverbial notion that if the fathers ate sour grapes, the children would pay the consequences.[16]

Herodotus tells an amazing tale concerning Hecataeus (who traced his ancestry back sixteen generations to a god), that when he visited Thebes in Egypt the priests of Zeus there, not recognizing the descent of a human from a divine being, showed him the pedigree of their chief priests. The current priest claimed to be the last of a line of three hundred and forty-one generations of priests who had passed the office from father to son in unbroken succession. Each ancestor was represented by a tremendous wooden statue,

[15] Matt. 23:31; Luke 11:47-48; cf. Acts 7:51-53.
[16] Jer. 31:29; Ezek. 18:2.

erected during his lifetime.[17] This is but one example of evidence to show that the office of priest in many cults was hereditary. Josephus made the similarly extravagant claim that the high priesthood in Israel had passed from father to son without interruption for two thousand years back to Aaron.[18] The contention of the Qumran sectaries that the Jerusalem high priest was not the legitimate one and the recent discovery of a priestly genealogy in Cave 6 at Qumran show the importance attached to correctness of descent in that office.[19]

It is this function of genealogy that is predominant in the matter of restrictions imposed on matrimonial freedom by various groups in the ancient world. There were ancient laws in Rome and Athens regulating the marriage of citizens and prohibiting such marriage except within tne citizenry; otherwise the children of such marriages did not have the rights of citizenship. In the lists of Jewish families who came up from Babylonia after the Exile those who could not prove their father's house or their descent are given special mention, along with the sons of priests who could not find their families registered in the genealogies and were thus ineligible for the priesthood. Those who had married foreign wives were instructed to put them away.[20]

Josephus relates the precautions which must be taken when a priest marries. He must marry within his race and must investigate the ancestry of his bride from the public archives, all in order that he shall be eligible, as far as race and genealogy are concerned, to officiate in the temple. The phenomenon of brother-sister marriages among the Ptolemaic rulers of Egypt, which was of great antiquity and which later was practiced by commoners after the example of the king, may have been continued for a similar reason, to keep the divine blood of the ruler from contamination and thus to insure the eligibility of his son to the throne. For lack of "pure" Jewish background, Edomites, Samaritans, and Galileans were despised by their Jewish contemporaries. Nathaniel was not the only Jew who could have asked, "Can anything good come out of Nazareth?"[21] To his other unpopular qualities Herod added the unfortunate condition that he was only a "half-Jew."

In Judaism, the phrase "son of Abraham" conveyed a hint of

[17] Herodotus, *Hist.* ii. 143.

[18] *Apion* 1. 36.

[19] F. M. Cross, Jr., *The Ancient Library of Qumran* (London, 1958), pp. 96ff.; M. Burrows, *More Light on the Dead Sea Scrolls* (New York, 1958), Appendix.

[20] Ezra 2:59-63; Neh. 7:61-65; Ezra 10.

[21] John 1:46.

qualification as well as description. As a son of Abraham, according to ancient tradition, a Jew was an heir to the promises which Abraham had received. The resulting tendency to smugness on the part of Jews aroused the prophetic wrath of John the Baptist who warned that God could produce children of Abraham out of stones if he chose.[22] Likewise the phrase "son of David," originally meaning a descendant of David and a reigning king, came to stand for an office. For one to be so called meant in the popular mind that he was qualified for a unique role in the life of the Jewish people— that of a long-awaited ruler.

6. MOTIVATION AND INSPIRATION.—Finally, a genealogy might in certain instances have the function of inspiring a descendant to pattern his life after a worthy ancestor. Plutarch quotes an aphorism of Dionysodorus of Troezen: "Who will praise a father if not unhappy sons?" He regards this as the perfect squelch to those worthless descendants who are forever praising their ancestors but do nothing to measure up to them. Plutarch has written a life of Aratus for the benefit of Polycrates and Pythocles, two sons of his friend, in order that the memory of this great ancestor of theirs may be a stimulus to their own achievement.[23]

We turn now to the genealogies of Jesus and ask whether this enumeration of the roles of genealogy can aid in their interpretation. It will be clear at the outset that the function of motivation is not pertinent to our discussion. There is no sure indication that either of the pedigrees was known to Jesus' family or to him. The letter of Bishop Africanus to Aristides in the early third century records that somewhat before his time the δεσπόσυνοι (members of the family of Jesus, the δεσπότης) were disseminating the complicated harmonizing interpretation of the two genealogies.[24] According to them, says Africanus, the Matthean genealogy gave the descent according to *law* while the Lucan genealogy gave it according to *nature*. This assumption, plus the hypothesis of a levirate marriage, eliminated the most glaring difficulties in the way of harmonization and remained the prevailing interpretation in the Church for centuries. Africanus himself apparently found the argument somewhat unconvincing, but it was the best that he knew. At any rate, it shows that Jesus' relatives had no certain knowledge of their ancestry at this time. On the other hand, Paul believed Jesus to be, humanly speaking, a descendant of David, and this information he may

---

[22] Matt. 3:9.
[23] *Aratus* 12.
[24] Eusebius, *H. E.* i. 7.

have received from Jesus' brother James.[25] The only hint concerning Jesus' own opinion of his Davidic ancestry is that he did not take it very seriously.[26]

With regard to the function of identification, each genealogy fits Jesus into a wider community of kinship—Matthew's to the Jewish people, Luke's to the entire human race. Elsewhere in the Gospels he is spoken of as "Jesus son of Joseph" and in other terms expressive of family relationship.[27]

To the extent that a lengthy pedigree of itself conferred distinction on the bearer, the genealogies exhibit magnification. The presence of many celebrated names in each of them makes this the more probable. Whether they were composed with this purpose in view, however, is impossible to determine. There may have been people living in the first century for whom reading one of these genealogies for the first time helped to a markedly heightened appreciation of Jesus. We must assume that such a reader understood what he read as a genealogy of Jesus, and that he did not feel the conflict which a modern reader is likely to feel in the fact that it is just these Gospels which also set forth the tradition of a supernatural birth.

We proceed now to an examination of the separate genealogies. The Gospel according to Matthew, and thus the New Testament as a whole, begins with a genealogy, called a βίβλος γενέσεως,[28] of Jesus Christ, who is further characterized as son of David and son of Abraham. Then follows a line of descent which specifies in just what way Jesus is entitled to these designations. The line proceeds from father to son, beginning with Abraham, the father of all Jews, continuing to David, the beloved king of Israel, through the dynasty he founded, and after the Exile through a series of unknown and unsung descendants, most of whom are important only as links in a continuous chain.

As far as the names can be controlled by I Chronicles, there are only minor difficulties, such as the omission of three kings, Joash, Amaziah and Uzziah at verse 9, the confusion of Jehoiakim and Jechoniah at verse 11, and the parentage of Zerubbabel (who is called Pedaiah in I Chron. 3:19 but Shealtiel or Salathiel in Ezra and Nehemiah). At the last generation of the pedigree the pattern is altered, so that the emphasis is upon the maternity of Mary rather than the paternity of Joseph. This verse (16) has many variant forms of text, some, such as the Sinaitic Syriac reading,

---

[25] Rom. 1:3; Gal. 1:18.
[26] Matt. 22:41-46; Mark 12:35-37; Luke 20:41-44.
[27] John 1:46, 6:42; Matt. 13:55-56; Mark 6:3; Luke 4:22.
[28] Cf. Gen. 5:1 (LXX).

tending to represent Joseph as unquestionably the father, others harmonizing better with the belief in a virgin birth of Jesus.[29] None of these readings, however, actually denies the paternity of Joseph. They simply assert the importance of Mary, who figured more importantly than Joseph in the life of Jesus and in early Christian memory.

The distinctiveness of the Matthean genealogy lies in the numerical pattern which it exhibits and in the added touches of a historical or biographical character. Alongside the names of nine ancestors—Jacob, Judas, Salmon, Boaz, Jesse, David, Josiah, Jechoniah, and Joseph—are some additional comments. Five of these refer to women, who are not ordinarily mentioned.[30] One mentions the brothers of Judah, the eponymous ancestors of the twelve tribes of Israel; one mentions David specifically as king; one mentions another set of brothers, perhaps considered as progenitors of separate branches of the house of David; and one calls particular attention to the $\mu\epsilon\tauοικεσία$ $Βαβυλῶνος$. The presence of these comments shows that we have here not a bare genealogy but a brief history written in the genealogical manner, preparing the reader for the gospel narrative to follow by tracing the background of the story. As such, the function of organization is prominent, as is made even more evident by verse 17.

The division of the genealogy into three groups of fourteen generations each accounts for some of the difficulties and gives a clue to the author's purpose. It accounts probably for the omission of the three kings in verse 9 and the dropping out of Jehoiakim in verse 11. This was probably done to keep the number of generations in that group down to fourteen. The number fourteen is the numerical value of the letters of the name David in Hebrew, thus possibly suggesting Jesus as triply, that is, superlatively, Davidic. However, only thirteen names are given in the third division of the genealogy. Various hypotheses have been advanced to account for this defect. Probably the simplest explanation is that in the third division both first and last names are counted. From Jechoniah to Jesus, inclusive,

---

[29] A. H. McNeile, *The Gospel According to St. Matthew* (London, 1915), p. 4, has a convenient collection of the principal variants.

[30] Whether the non-Israelite Tamar, the Canaanite Rahab, the Moabite Ruth and the wife of the Hittite are to be understood as parallels to Mary and thus hint at a non-Jewish origin for her, cannot be proved. In any case, the scandal of adultery associated with three of them does not seem to have been emphasized in Jewish tradition. Rahab, the heroine of faith (Heb. 11:31) and of works (James 2:25), was revered also as ancestress of several prophets. As such, she is a fitting ancestress for Jesus, the prophet *par excellence*.

there are fourteen generations.[31] This three-fold division makes for chronological difficulties, since on any reckoning the average generation is over forty years in length, and about forty-seven years if only thirteen generations are counted. But the difficulty is more apparent to the modern reader than to a first-century audience, for whom chronology was not an exact science.

What the Matthean genealogy succeeds in doing is to represent the history of the Jewish people as separated into three sharply defined periods. In the first, the Jewish nation came into being and developed without benefit of the institution of the monarchy. In the second, Israel flourished as a monarchy, under the sway of successive members of the House of David, in conformity with the promises made to David and repeated to his descendants. In the third period, initiated by the deportation of the cream of the Jewish people to Babylon, Israel was again without a king and subject to foreigners. The interlude of independence under the Hasmoneans is passed over without comment. Now, with the birth of Jesus the kingdom is about to be restored, and the long-held hopes of Israel are, in the writer's view, nearing fulfillment.

The remainder of the Gospel continues to reflect this interest in the monarchy. The birth of Jesus coincides with the announcement by a star to magi in the distant East. They come to offer him their gifts and their devotion. Herod "the king" is gravely upset to hear that one has been *born* king of the Jews—that there is one who is qualified for the kingship by virtue of his royal descent. Herod shows by his anxiety that he is not the legitimate ruler.

Jesus' ministry is foreshadowed by John's announcement that the *Kingdom of Heaven* is close at hand (3:2). Jesus' first proclamation is to the same effect (4:17), and when Jesus sends out his disciples, he instructs them to make the same announcement (10:7). Jesus' teaching is preoccupied with the character of the Kingdom of God. He sees his countrymen as lost and wayward sheep, needing a shepherd. As the shepherd David became shepherd of Israel, so Jesus is the needed shepherd. The proclamation of the Kingdom is made to the lost sheep of the house of Israel. When the time comes, Jesus enters Jerusalem the city of the great king, as a king, in' over-literal fulfillment of the words of the prophet Zechariah (9:9),

---

[31] A quite different view of the three "fourteens" is offered by E. J. Goodspeed, who argues that this pattern is to exhibit Jesus as the beginning of the seventh seven since Abraham, thus representing the "climax of history." Goodspeed also believes that this numerical interest marks the author as Matthew the tax collector, the man of figures. *Matthew, Apostle and Evangelist* (Philadelphia, 1959), p. 25.

just as throughout his life one detail after another is shown to be a fulfillment of ancient prophecy and thus all part of a divine plan. The genealogy suggests that the whole history of Israel is a part of the divine plan. From the question of the magi to Herod, to the question of Pilate to the condemned Jesus, to the inscription placed upon the cross, to the final declaration of the risen Christ that all authority in heaven and earth is his, Jesus plays the part of king. The genealogy legitimizes this kingly role.

The Lucan genealogy by comparison is much simpler in structure and, from the point of view of length, more impressive. Unlike the Matthean line, this one begins with Jesus and proceeds from son to father. Here also there is some uncertainty about the genealogy, because of the phrase ὡς ἐνομίζετο before the name Joseph (3:23). There is no textual support for supposing that the phrase is an interpolation, and it is often thought that the writer inserted it in order to soften the conflict between the genealogy and the tradition of a virgin birth of Jesus.[32] However, the genealogy is meaningless in its gospel context unless it is intended to refer to Jesus. Used in the passive voice, the verb νομίζω can refer to what is habitual or customary, as it does in one reading of Acts 16:13. Thus a plausible translation of the verse is:"Jesus as he was beginning (his ministry) was about thirty years old, being the son, *as his genealogy was ordinarily reckoned*, of Joseph, the son of Heli." Thus the use of the phrase may be simply the author's way of protecting himself from seeming to vouch for a pedigree of seventy-seven generations, without implying that he personally rejected it. The real crux of interpretation is the subject of the verb ἐνομίζετο. Does it refer to the possibility that Jesus was the son of Joseph or that Jesus had this entire pedigree? Since it is often assumed throughout the Gospel that Joseph is the father,[33] that would not seem to be the point in question.

The fact that the Lucan genealogy goes all the way back to Adam and God has often been understood as an indication of Luke's "universalism." This appears possible, especially when we read Luke in the light of Matthew. However, there is no evidence that Luke is consciously opposing Matthew and it is much easier to assume that the two Gospels reflect different backgrounds. The names in Matthew and Luke largely coincide between Abraham and David, but differ in the generations between David and Joseph,

[32] Cf. Luke 1:4.
[33] Luke 2:5, 16, 22, 27, 33, 40, 48; 4:22.

except for Zerubbabel and his father Salathiel.[34] The name Rhesa, the "son" of Zerubbabel, probably represents a misunderstanding of the Aramaic word for prince and should stand in apposition to Zerubbabel. The inclusion of a second *Cainan* in verse 36 shows probably the influence of the Septuagint. The tracing of Jesus through Nathan rather than Solomon may have been promoted by the curse of Jeremiah against Jechoniah, of whom he wrote that none of his offspring should succeed him on the throne of David (22:24, 30). Nathan is represented as an elder brother of Solomon in some passages, and his family is mentioned as a branch of the house of David.[35]

By comparison with Matthew, the Lucan genealogy seems less artificial. However, the seventy-seven generations can be grouped in sevens, such that the first name in a group is often one of importance. Thus Jesus begins the first heptad, Joseph the second, another Jesus the fifth, another Joseph the sixth, David the seventh, Abraham the ninth, and Enoch the eleventh.

But the purpose of the genealogy is best understood in connection with its setting in the Gospel. It follows immediately the baptismal narrative, at the end of which a voice from heaven declares, "This is my beloved son. . . ." Anyone who reads this as a statement of a genealogical character would be interested in knowing in just what way Jesus was the son of God. Luke's gentile readers (such as Theophilus) would be familiar with pedigrees by which leading families and individuals and religious figures such as heroes were traced to one of the gods. At the end of such a pedigree there would be a last human ancestor, who would be biologically a son of god. The phrase, Ἀδὰμ τοῦ Θεοῦ at the end of Luke's genealogy is awkward from the standpoint of Jewish thinking if it means biological descent of Adam from God, but it would pose no such problem for a Greek. Thus we may take the entire genealogy as an attempt to elucidate the saying of the voice from heaven which was heard at the baptism.

Such an interpretation is complicated by the fact that in a number of western manuscripts[36] the voice from heaven utters a quotation of Ps. 2:7, *Thou art my son, today I have begotten thee.* If we emphasize

[34] It is entirely natural that both genealogies should include Zerubbabel, that leader among the returning exiles who was to be God's signet ring and chosen one, who was expected to receive the crown and the throne of Israel— Hagg. 2:23; Zech. 6:9-14 (reading Zerubbabel for Joshua in verse 11).

[35] II Sam. 5:14; I Chron. 3:5; 14:14; Zech. 12:12. See G. Kuhn, "Die Geschlechts-register Jesus bei Lukas und Matthäus," *ZNW*, XXII (1923), 206 ff.

[36] D, a, b, and others; Augustine, Justin, Clement.

the word "today," the genealogy is again meaningless. We observe, however, that the quotation is from one of the "Royal" psalms and referred originally to the accession of a king. If this is the original reading, the implication is that the voice from heaven announces the accession of Jesus to his own ministry, an interpretation which is strengthened by the participle ἀρχόμενος in the following verse. The phrase σήμερον γεγέννηκά σε may then have been understood as an official endorsement of Jesus, with the genealogy following to show how Jesus was, and had been all along, the son of God.[37]

Thus the primary purpose of the Lucan genealogy is to exhibit Jesus as the son of God. This is done in a manner which makes him son of Zerubbabel, son of David, and son of Abraham as well. By stating his descent from God in terms of his descent from Adam, the writer does not answer the question in what way Jesus differs from other men. According to Jewish tradition, all men were sons of Adam, and this common kinship is recognized by the writer in Acts 17:28 in words presumably familiar to Paul's Athenian audience: τοῦ γὰρ καὶ γένος ἐσμέν. The only distinction accorded to Jesus is that he has here his complete line of descent from Adam, whereas most human beings are without a written genealogy.

An apparently conflicting attitude toward genealogy as applied to Jesus is found in Hebrews. Here the passage at Ps. 110:4 is applied frequently to Christ, and the correspondence is carefully worked out. Melchizedek, the mysterious figure of Gen. 14, who was king of Salem, or king of peace, by etymology also king of righteousness, is ἀπάτωρ, ἀμήτωρ, ἀγενεαλόγητος, having neither beginning nor end to his life but resembling the son of God (that is, Christ) continuing forever as priest.[38] The resemblance between Jesus and Melchizedek is in their *eternal* priesthood, as opposed to the temporary and provisional Levitical priesthood. It is not implied that Jesus had neither father nor mother nor genealogy. He had them all by implication, for he was descended from the tribe of Judah.[39] Jesus' priesthood is non-Levitical, for he has become priest not because of his family qualifications but "by the power of an indestructible (and hence eternal) life." Melchizedek, on the other hand, is non-Levitical precisely because of his lack of genealogical requirements, not to mention that he antedated Levi by about

---

[37] It is significant that D, which is the principal Greek MS representing this reading, has between Joseph and David the names of Matthew 1:6-16 in reverse order. Here, at least, Jesus, to whom the voice quoted the royal psalm, is of the royal line.

[38] Heb. 5:6, 10; 6:20; 7:1-17.

[39] Heb. 7:14.

three generations. The chief interest in the passage for our investigation is in what it reveals concerning genealogy as a means of qualification. Here lack of genealogy can render a person ineligible (for the Levitical priesthood).[40]

In late Judaism and early Christianity alike, it was taken for granted that God was a living God, who, to use a modern phrase, was active in history. This activity could be conceived in two principal ways. In the first place, God could intervene directly in the affairs of men. Thus he spoke to the fathers by the prophets and otherwise influenced history through miraculous events. But he could also act indirectly, through the working out of forces set in motion in the past. Thus an ancient blessing or curse or prophecy or promise could have far-reaching and continuing effect. In Jesus, early Christians saw evidence of the activity of God in both these aspects. On the one hand, God had sent him into the world and had worked directly through him. On the other hand, his coming was understood as the fruition of a divine plan, prepared long in advance. This idea of preparation could be expressed in many ways, but one of them is exemplified in Matthew and Luke in their giving us together, each in characteristically independent fashion, the genealogies of Jesus.

[40] An appendix to the Book of the Secrets of Enoch contains (3:1-21) a long episode concerning the supernatural birth of Melchizedek. He was born shortly after the death of his mother Sopanima, the wife of Nir, the brother of Noah. Sopanima had conceived in her old age without help from her husband, had died, and was prepared for burial when a child came forth from her and sat on the bed, fully developed as a three-year-old. Nir and Noah, terrified, named him Melchizedek. The story is of Christian provenance, having similarities to the virgin birth story of Jesus. It seems to be an ingenious attempt to show how Melchizedek could have had neither mother nor father nor genealogy.

II | *Albert Barnett*
EMORY UNIVERSITY

JESUS AS THEOLOGIAN

Authentic knowledge of the career and message of Jesus depends almost entirely on the canonical Gospels. These Gospels incorporate approximately everything about Jesus which the first-century church regarded as important. The character of the tradition they enshrine requires critical evaluation as the initial step in any discussion of what Jesus taught. Accordingly, the present essay on "Jesus as Theologian" is prefaced by a statement of the author's judgment of the validity of the gospel record.

The Fourth Gospel was the culmination of the gospel-making process. To regard it, however, as of the same character as the Synoptics is misleading and essentially fallacious. It is more than an advanced form of the process out of which all four canonical Gospels emerged. It is essentially a new employment of the gospel form, and as such must be distinguished from the three earlier illustrations of that form.

The authors of all four Gospels were missionary preachers, evangelists rather than biographers. What they wrote was a form of preaching, not history for its own sake. The Synoptics do not differ from the Fourth Gospel in this respect. The stimulation and support of faith was their common objective. The Synoptics resemble one another and differ from the Fourth Gospel, however, in that they were compilations of materials from older written sources, which in turn were crystallizations of oral tradition that had achieved a considerable degree of fixity during the twenty years immediately following the Crucifixion.

The Fourth Evangelist metamorphosed instead of reproducing the tradition. He meditated profoundly on older materials and in the Gospel he presented his own formulations of meaning rather

16

than the tradition that stimulated his reflections. The Synoptics are accordingly the principal reliance of historians.

The tradition underlying the three earlier Gospels is generally regarded as having been composed of small, self-contained units. The finished Gospels clearly indicate as much. Investment of the materials with such forms as pronouncement stories, miracle stories, stories about Jesus, and summaries of sayings was largely the methodology of the earliest pedagogy. Their correlation in the comprehensive presentations of the canonical Gospels was the achievement of the Evangelists. Selection and arrangement of traditional and widely familiar materials marked these men as authors in the truest sense. In the highly individual selection and arrangement of materials, the message of each Evangelist in his own immediate situation is to be found.

Crucial differences of scholarly opinion grow out of divergent judgments of the primary character of the elements that compose the evangelic tradition. The Gospels may be regarded as affording no certain knowledge of Jesus and his teaching because the tradition they enshrine had its only genesis in early Christian preaching. They illuminate the growth of Christian thought and are a phase of the history of the Church, but they provide the historian with no dependable information about Jesus. Only what first-century heralds thought of him remains. The teaching of Jesus, on this basis, is removed from discussion; the teaching of the early church makes up the gospel record.

The more probable view historically is that the tradition about Jesus itself gave rise to preaching and became the content of the message of early evangelists and teachers. Selective memory, not creative imagination based on visual experiences, determined what missionary preachers proclaimed. Tradition owed its origin and growth to the Church in the sense that practical usefulness in evangelism and Christian nurture determined what was preserved in memory and later transmitted in literature.

In this latter view, the Gospels, their written sources, and the antecedent oral tradition reflect but did not originate Christian interest in Jesus' historical career and message. He was personally remembered and the allegiance of the first disciples was to him as their Master. He was more definitely a leader than a teacher. Task took precedence over teaching with him and teaching was the form of action dictated by the character of his objectives. His words were remembered, therefore, not because they were unprecedented so much as because he said them. They bore the imprint of his personality and objectives, and commitment to his leadership and goals caused his words to be treasured. He was never forgotten, and the tradition of his words affords the historian a substantially dependable account of the kind of person he was, the values he exalted, the objectives for whose actualization he lived and died.

Though written relatively late, the canonical Gospels were enlargements of earlier and less extensive documents, and these were related to oral tradition whose substance was based on first-hand testimony. The first readers of these Gospels had long been familiar with the materials they incorporated and would normally have objected to versions too radically different from accepted accounts. Precisely that disposition made acceptance of the Fourth Gospel difficult and put such acceptance off until well into the second century.

The tradition of Jesus' teaching was probably the oldest and most authentic element in oral and written accounts of his career. Its origin and character hardly warrants skepticism of its reliability. Where skepticism exists, it is the outgrowth of conclusions about the character of the Gospels.

On that basis, Paul, the Fourth Evangelist, and the unknown author of Hebrews are the theologians of the New Testament.[1] If the canonical Gospels are differently evaluated, however, Jesus himself becomes more probably the creator of the theological substructure of the New Testament. On foundations he established, the admittedly original minds of Paul, the Fourth Evangelist, and the author of Hebrews worked creatively, each in his distinctive way. Such is the suggestion of the title of this essay, "Jesus as Theologian."

Jesus' teaching as contained in the Synoptics is less miscellaneous than is sometimes supposed. It is closely knit and coherent rather than chaotic. It contains an integrating principle of which its several phases are expositions. Underlying all particular things Jesus said is the theological premise of God's providence. God is viewed as caring individually for persons. Men may, therefore, count with confidence on God's love and guidance and thereby live by his will. His knowledge and power come to focus in his administration of creation in the interest of the welfare of persons. God's providence is thus the basis of religion for Jesus, and in this doctrine of providence is rooted the treatment of all particular themes. His life and message were predicated on this conviction of God's paternal concern, and both are best interpreted as expressions of that conviction.

[1] R. Bultmann *Theology of the New Testament*, tr. by Kendrick Grobel (New York, 1951), Vol. 1.

Jesus made no attempt to blueprint life. He looked to God for daily guidance and taught his followers so to do. His attitude was the antithesis of legalism, and his radical rejection of legalism gave Paul a precedent for his comparable disposition. Throughout his career, Jesus waited on God for guidance in the use of his life. That is the explanation of his frequent and lengthy periods of prayer.

Jesus did not arrive at his view of providence by abstract reasoning. It grew out of his religious consciousness. His sense of God involved profound trustfulness. He entrusted his life to God's hands, constantly sought his guidance, and experienced the peace and power of such commitment. His view of providence and the process of its achievement were not new in the sense of having no precedents. The Old Testament contained magnificent illustrations. In some degree, it is universally implicit in religion, because religion consists in the conviction of the existence of a Higher Power to whom men cannot be indifferent and toward whom they can hardly be independent. Prayer is the central feature of vital religion, and prayer rests on some sort of faith in providence.

Such newness as Jesus' doctrine of providence had grew out of the unique intensity and realism of his trustfulness. In his thought God's care expressed itself in direct concern for persons as such, rather than as members of an elect race or holy nation. Righteousness, not special privilege, determined God's judgment and radical, equalitarian democracy supplanted any sort of aristocratic status. Every human soul, in its own right, had a place in God's fatherly love. God knew and cared for men one by one. On this basis the last, the least, the lost among men had dignity and worth.

Jesus made little effort to establish his position by reasoned argument; he thought that its exposition was sufficient commendation. Insofar as he reasoned about it, he employed analogies from nature. There, he found God caring for needs. The world existed because its Creator was actuated by love. His beneficent will and infinite wisdom created the beauty and sense of duty that gave the world meaning and order. Nature supplied analogies for religious insight but was not its inspiration. Jesus' faith arose from a vivid sense of guidance from God and of constant fellowship with God. These were its proofs. They determined decisions and measured the intensity and reality of religious experience. The rigorous demands Jesus made on his disciples were the corollaries of his religious devotion.

At five principal points, Jesus' view of providence determined his teaching. It made anxiety unwarranted; it was the basis of devotion to spiritual values; it justified patience; it inspired courage;

it confirmed the hope of immortality. Because God knows and cares for men as individuals, men need not worry. Favorable or adverse circumstances mattered little. The mood of quiet trust was a source of strength. The future was better assured by courageous confidence than by skeptical timidity. Willingness to live one day at a time on the premise that God's power was guided by his individualized love for persons made uncertainty about detailed and immediate consequences of little importance. This, for Jesus, was good sense; anxiety accomplished only distraction and weakness.

Freedom from anxiety enabled men to devote themselves to spiritual values. They could expect God's help only if their lives were devoted to godly goals. God's approval was conditioned on the enshrinement of spiritual values in the human heart. Commitment to spiritual values reduced to a minimum men's need for material things, and for that minimum they could count confidently on God. This faith involved no encouragement of idleness or mendicancy. The dismissal of paralyzing fears rather generated effectiveness in achievement and a capacity for the highest concentration on immediate tasks, since results were God's province.

Patience for Jesus meant expectant waiting on God. It involved no trace of lethargy or inertia. It was not an acquiescence in injustice, but rather the religious alternative to the assumption that man is himself the world's only providence. It was actually a mood of action. It consisted in the steady and persistent activity on behalf of good ends warranted by the faith that God is himself on the side of right and that success for the right is therefore possible. Good causes are never lost causes, because of God's power and wisdom. Pride and limited vision tempt men to assume to lead God or to force his hand. Preferably, for Jesus, men should do God's will day by day with no diminution of self-exertion, take the next step as he reveals it and count on God for results. Jesus' conduct of his own life illuminates the meaning of the patience his words commend.

Courage was not relinquished to paganism. Jesus thought that true godliness required and inspired the highest quality of courage. A realistic assumption that God's power supports the man who wills to do the divine will afforded true security, however adverse immediate circumstances might appear. That conviction set the Christian standard for courage. It made possible an abandonment of fear of nature, circumstance, and society. Boldness and initiative were encouraged and abundantly warranted. By providing a religious basis for courage, Jesus made the little people of the world courageous and established for courage a higher quality than the world had previously known.

Prayer in its most meaningful richness was inspired by Jesus' assurance that God is solicitous about the needs of men and is himself eager for fellowship and collaboration with men. Prayer for Jesus was not a matter of insistent petition so much as an alert waiting for God to speak. Sincerity and trustfulness prepared the praying person to hear God speak and to accept his guidance. Discovery of the divine will and way, not the imposition of man's preferences, was the true goal in prayer. The major premise of prayer for Jesus was that God knew the needs of men better than any man and that he knew these needs without being told. Prayer was thus neither a matter of informing nor of persuading God. God's omniscience combined with his infinite love made prayer a way of discovery and a means whereby the entire life might be disciplined to obey the truth when clearly apprehended. The renewal and empowering of the will for utter obedience was for Jesus the end result of prayer.

Finally, Jesus' doctrine of providence justified and greatly sharpened man's hope of immortality. Jesus claimed no specific knowledge of the after-life and discussed it with great reserve. His position was essentially that man's future is hidden with God, howbeit a God who cares for men individually with a father's devotion. God's love was constant and eternal, not occasional and temporary. On this basis, he urged men to serve God faithfully and courageously each day and assume that God would make the future what it ought to be. He felt that the issues of daily life had eternal bearings. At the same time obedience under earthly conditions was faulty and fellowship with God limited. If, under such conditions, men devoted themselves to God's will, they might justifiably look forward to a future in which fellowship would be perfected and obedience unconditioned by earthly hindrances.

Jesus' interest was more definitely in the moral quality of life than in survival for its own sake. The future life, therefore, held the promise of a richer goodness and a more faithful likeness to God. Thus he correlated the hope of personal survival with moral values and religious faith. Confidence in God's love and goodness was the starting point. He reasoned from God's character that he would provide for men's needs beyond earthly existence just as he had within the sphere of man's existence in time.

The conviction that God's love would know no lapse controlled Jesus' view of life beyond death. To be loved with God's eternal love gives eternal quality and meaning to human life. This explains the conviction that God is the God of the living, not of the dead, of Abraham, Isaac, and Jacob. A realistic and vital relation to God nullifies the fear of death. This was the essential meaning of Pauline predestination: God predestined men "to be conformed to the image of his Son, in order that he might be the first born among many brethren . . . . For God consigned all men to disobedience, that he might have mercy upon all" (Rom. 8:29 ff.; 11:32-38).

The eternity of moral values contributed also to Jesus' thought about future life. Such values endure, and life devoted to these values endures. Jesus' ethic was not conceived as a way of life for an interim of any sort. Men were called on to live by the ethic of eternity. So to live would constitute their contribution to the inauguration of God's Kingdom on earth and would at the same time be the badge of citizenship in that Kingdom. The Kingdom of God was thus the realm of eternal values. Earthly and temporal values decay, but no change affects or causes the disintegration of love, truth, goodness. The man whose will is one with God's will is thus assured immortality. For such a person, physical death becomes incidental.

God's individualized love for persons, the worth of every person to God, the eternity of spiritual values make the theological position of Jesus intelligible and relevant for the twentieth century. It is in such terms that theology is best formulated today. Discussing the question, "Does Civilization Still Need Religion?," William E. Hocking said not too long ago,

> How do you read the history of western civilization? The essence of it is not that it has bred science and technique, nor that it has bred laws and a high civic order. The essence of it is that it has bred men; and that men have produced the sciences and the public order. How has it bred men? Here our sociologists customarily go blind and appeal to mechanical psychology, or northern climates, or nordic races, or inventions, or movements of populations, or rise of capital wealth . . . . The central thing is that men have lived with all their usual problems and energies and passions, under the spell of a religion which encouraged them to believe in their own worth, not in each other's natural eyes, but in the eyes of an absolute and competent judge of worth. They had a God who cared for them, not indulgently and mushily but with a divine and severe insight."[2]

---

[2] *Christendom*, Vol. I (1935), p. 39.

Thus may the twentieth century adapt Jesus' view of providence. In that adaptation lies the promise of the most creative solutions of problems common to mankind, however the forms of the problems may vary with the times.

III | *Carl H. Kraeling*

UNIVERSITY OF CHICAGO

SEEK AND YOU WILL FIND

Matthew 7	Luke 11
7 Ask, and it will be given you; seek, and you will find; knock, and it will be opened to you. 8 For everyone who asks receives, and he who seeks finds, and to him who knocks it will be opened.	9 . . . Ask, and it will be given you; seek, and you will find; knock and it will be opened to you. 10 For every one who asks receives, and he who seeks finds, and to him who knocks it will be opened.
9 Or what man of you, if his son asks him for a loaf, will give him a stone?	11 What father among you, if his son asks for a fish, will instead of a fish give him a serpent;
10 Or if he asks for a fish, will give him a serpent?	12 or if he asks for an egg, will give him a scorpion?
11 If you then, who are evil, know how to give good gifts to your children, how much more will your Father who is in heaven give good things to those who ask him?	13 If you then, who are evil, know how to give good gifts to your children, how much more will the heavenly Father give the Holy Spirit to those who ask him?

The doubly-attested logion in which the proverbial "seek and you will find" occurs and which is here given in full for convenience' sake in the rendering of the Revised Standard Version is among the more familiar of the sayings of Jesus. Quoted and commented upon by Christian writers since the days of the earliest anti-heretical Fathers and speculative theologians, it is still subject to interpretation from different points of view and does in fact raise various questions. So, for instance, it is interesting to inquire in what context the saying may have stood in the Second Source from which Matthew and Luke drew it; that is, whether it was handed down as one element of a collection of words dealing with prayer and the answer to prayer such as Luke 11:1-13, and if so why Matthew chose to take it out of that context and to incorporate it in the somewhat hetero-geneous terminal section of the Sermon on the Mount? Similarly, it is interesting to ask whether, if the Lucan context is the older, the reference to the giving of the Holy Spirit in the Lucan version should be credited only to Luke's well-known interest in the coming and the working of the Spirit, or whether the reference should be credited to the Second Source because it prepares the way for the statement about the driving out of the evil spirits in the Beelzebul Controversy that follows in Luke 11:14-20? In the same way one can speculate whether in the Second Source the logion contained three rhetorical questions (about the "loaf" and the "stone," the "fish" and the "serpent," and the "egg" and the "scorpion" respectively) of which Matthew and Luke each chose to bring only two, or whether the earlier version had only two rhetorical questions and, if so, which two? Finally, it can be argued whether the opening injunctions ("ask," "seek," "knock") and the rhetorical questions that follow do not together represent the primitive core of the saying? The concluding words ("If you then . . ."), even though they are as old as the Second Source, would then be a Christian application developed in the process of transmission, and those Church Fathers who found in the relative clause "you, who are evil" confirmation of the Pauline doctrine of original sin would have been on the right track after all.

The discussion of these and other similar questions is the proper prerogative of the New Testament scholar, dealing as he is with a body of documentary evidence and having from this scanty material to reconstruct an intelligible and reasonable interpretation of the development of the tradition they contain. And indeed all who wish to use these documents for historical purposes will need to pay heed to and make their choice among the answers given to these scholarly questions, for no one can safely judge historical probabilities without an adequate knowledge of the development of his source material. But this type of discussion, important as it is for critical judgment, often stops short of the effort to penetrate to the essential core of a given piece of historical material, and in so doing not only leaves the general reader disappointed but also deprives itself of the valuable help that perspective can give in any reconstruction of the process of transmission. One might expect that the works of the more practically-minded commentators would help overcome the de-ficiencies of critical interpretation in such cases, but they tend instead to be sterile and unimaginative. So, for instance, the "Exegesis" section of the page devoted to Matt. 7:7-11 in the *Interpreter's Bible* (1951, p. 328) offers as the sum total of its comment on our saying the statement that "a loaf is shaped somewhat like a stone, and fish like a serpent." In P. A. Micklem's "St. Matthew" in the *Westminster Commentary* (1917, p. 66) it also appears, and the chances are that like so many of the 'old chestnuts' handed down in successive New Testament commentaries, this interpretation derives ultimately from the famous *Gnomon* of J. A. Bengel, where a century ago students who of course could read Latin found it said : *pani extrinsecus similis est lapis . . .; et pisci, anguis. . . .*

Anyone inclined on such grounds to bemoan the apparent lack of progress in New Testament interpretation during the past hundred years would soon find himself confronted with the question from what sources he would draw the supplementary information needed to overcome such deficiencies. The question is a fair one and the answer is that very often the information needed actually exists, but that it comes from areas of knowledge and experience outside the sphere in which the Bible student tends to work. So, for instance, in the case of the "Seek, and you will find" logion it can be said that some direct acquaintance with life in the Near East, both in the more traditional aspects of its contemporary manifestation and in what can be learned from archeology, and some familiarity with non-biblical documentary and monumental source materials will provide what is needed to make the core of the saying and its development more intelligible.

The simple and very obvious key to an understanding of the "Seek and you will find" saying is the fact that it paints a vignette of family life at its simplest level in the Palestine of Jesus' day. What is needed for an interpretation of the saying and its development is some knowledge of the setting and of the procedure of this family life. The setting is clearly one of the small, largely agricultural hamlets of Galilee in which Jesus was so much at home and which, regrettably, are still so imperfectly documented in archeological record. But the type will be quite familiar to anyone who has lived or moved about in the more remote villages of the contemporary Near East that, save for the presence of the *abu-benzine* (the fuel pump), remain relatively untouched by western civilization, and to anyone who is familiar with the results of the excavations at Beth-Zur, Tell beit Mirsim and Bethel in Palestine, with what is known about Ptolemaic and Roman private houses from the Greek papyri of Egypt and with what we have learned about domestic establishments in later Mesopotamia from the excavations at Assur, Seleucia on the Tigris and Dura-Europos.[1]

---

[1] See O. R. Sellers, *The Citadel of Beth-Zur* (Philadelphia 1933); W. F. Albright

Typically the agricultural hamlet of Jesus' Galilee was a rather drab and unimpressive collection of one-story, flat-roofed dwellings crowded together in a minimum of space and with a minimum of attention to regularity of inner and outer arrangement. Narrow alleys giving access to the several establishments thread their way between them, flanked on either side by windowless house-walls. In Palestine these walls commonly have a core or a foundation and base of undressed stones heavily bedded in mud mortar and are finished on the outside with a coating of mud, chopped straw and manure that hardens in the strong heat of the sun and holds together even when softened by the winter's rains. Low rectangular openings, one to each house, provide the only breaks in the vertical faces of the trough-like alleys. A stone or two set in the front of them acts as a sill and keeps the rainwater from draining into the houses. A crude wooden frame set into the doorway supports an ill-fitting assembly of boards that represents the door. Inside lies an irregular open area, a courtyard, enclosed by similar mud-coated walls that partition the premises into rooms, each lighted only by its open doorways. The rooms are low, small, unadorned, and the poles that support the wickerwork bedding for the flat mud roof extend slightly out over the courtyard to keep the rainwater from running down the walls.

The courtyard is the scene of much of the family life. It is here that the cooking is done, frequently in an alcove under a mud staircase leading up to the roof of the main chamber where one sleeps in the heat of the summer and where reserves of dung and brush for fuel are stored. It is here that water is drawn from the cistern into which the rainwater from the roofs drains in winter. Such flattish stones as have turned up in the building or rebuilding of the walls provide firm and relatively dry footing for passage across the court when the rains create puddles here and there and make its unpaved surface slippery. Here the greens cut in the fields for the household's donkey are daily thrown down and consumed; here the occasional chicken scratches and squawks, here the children sit and play, and here the queries, the complaints, and the com-

---

"The Excavations of Tell Beit Mirsim III, The Iron Age," in *Annual of the American Schools of Oriental Research*, XXI-XXII (1943); the final reports on Professor J. A. Kelso's excavations at Bethel have not yet appeared; on Egypt see e.g., F. Luckhard, "Das Privathaus im ptolemäischen und römischen Ägypten Assur," in *Wissenschaftliche Veröffentlichungen der deutschen Orientgesellschaft*, LVII (1933). Material on the private houses at Seleucia is currently being prepared for publication; on private houses at Dura-Europos see *The Excavations at Dura-Europos, Preliminary Report* V, (New Haven, 1934), esp. pp. 31-34.

mands of family conversation and intercourse echo in the simple
pattern of daily life. Nothing is regular, nothing is tended; a weed
can flourish in a corner there, a mouse can have a nest under a
fodder-crib here, a spider or a garden-snake can have a hole yonder.
The daily round of taking care of the essential necessities is too
exacting to permit of concern for the modification of such circumstances.

What we read in the introductory section (Matt. 7:7-8 and Luke
11:9-10) of our logion as a series of injunctions with the key words
"seek," "knock" and "ask," can readily be combined with what is
said in the rhetorical questions about the father and his son (Matt.
7:9-10 and Luke 11:11-12) into a simple incident of family life,
typical in a hamlet such as that described. We are dealing with a
family that has a son grown to maturity, who has already established
himself outside the paternal home. Presumably he has a wife and
family of his own and he helps his father, who is already along in
years, by working in the field and tending the animals that need to
be pastured under personal supervision. But the all-important fact
is that the animals and the fields are still his father's and their
yield is his father's, so that when he needs something he must come
to his father and ask for it. So it is that in the vignette of the saying
we find the son coming down the alley that leads to his father's
house, evidently bent on an errand. He is "seeking" something. He
reaches the doorway of the parental home and "knocks," this being
an essential part of any visit to a domestic establishment where the
only privacy available is the privacy from those outside its walls.
The house door having been opened from within, father and son
meet in the courtyard of the house and it is there, after the filial
kiss and embrace, that the son "asks," as he must, for the simple
essentials of this day's sustenance. What the saying goes on to tell
us in the rhetorical questions (Matt. 7:9-10 and Luke 11:11-12)
and in the confident declarations (Matt. 7:8 and 11 and Luke 11:
10 and 13) about the father's possible and probable responses to the
son's requests, will be properly interpreted when attention is paid
not only to the locus of the action but also to the way of life and
thought in families of these agricultural hamlets.

In each of the two Gospels the rhetorical questions suggest two
requests on the part of the son and consider two responses that the
father might make and does not, but the requests and responses
are not identical. In Matthew the requests for a "loaf" and a "fish"
conjure up the possible response of the gift of a "stone" and a
"serpent," while in Luke the requests for a "fish" and an "egg"
provide the occasion for considering the propriety of the gift of a

"serpent" and a "scorpion." To decide whether all three questions are part of the original saying or only two, and if so which two, it is important to understand clearly the picture of the father that is implied in what he might do and actually does not do. In Luke the image of what the father might be, that is the image by comparison with which we get to understand his true nature, is perfectly clear. It is that of an inhuman and completely unnatural parent who, when confronted with a request for the most modest and the most readily and cheaply available means of sustenance, a "fish" and an "egg," responds by what the Evangelist must have regarded as the most noxious and harmful counterparts he could imagine, a poisonous "serpent" and an equally poisonous "scorpion." That any father could dream of so perverted a response to the request of his own son is horrible to contemplate, but it is clearly the intention of Luke to invoke precisely this horrible image as a foil to what a real father can be counted on to do. In Matthew, on the other hand, no unified picture of what the father might be, but is not, emerges. True, he might also give a "serpent" instead of a "fish," but his "stone" in place of a "loaf" is most innocuous and the cynical callousness with which his image might be charged on that score does not add force to the viciousness of his gift of a "serpent."

Faced as we are with the problem how many and which of the rhetorical questions to assign to the Second Source and to a hypothetical original logion, we can at least draw one inference from what has been said about the rejected father image. The inference, very simple, is that to project all three rhetorical questions back into the Second Source or into the original logion does not enhance the unity of the saying and is in fact in inverted form precisely the kind of conflation for which New Testament scholars so roundly condemn certain types of biblical texts and manuscripts. As between Matthew and Luke it should be obvious from what has been said that Luke has the more unified and consolidated rendering of the saying. In support of the claim that his version of the logion is the more primitive it can be argued that Jesus did on occasion use hyperbole, conjuring up drastic, unnatural pictures of potential human actions for the sake of effect, as when he spoke of "plucking out the eye" (Matt. 5:29) and of "cutting off the hand" (Matt. 18:8). But anyone with enough knowledge of the ancient scene to recognize our saying as a vignette of village life will hesitate to give the palm to the Lucan version for one elementary reason. It has lost contact with and has been turned aside from the circumstances of its setting. Monsters such as Luke's hypothetical father image are not typical of the agricultural villages of Galilee; neither are noxious "serpents" and vicious "scorpions" typical of the courtyards of simple dwellings.

Whether it is possible by considering the setting of the logion to arrive at a more acceptable interpretation of the saying depends on the appraisal of the Matthean version and of its value as a witness to the underlying tradition. In Matthew, it will be recalled, we have in the rhetorical questions about the father a picture of what he might be that is not consistent in itself. The potential response of the father suggested by the harmful gift of a "serpent" is out of harmony with the innocuous gift of a "stone." Is it possible and conceivable that in the pre-Matthean version of the saying the picture of what the father might be, but is not, was consistent but in a manner appropriate to the setting of the logion? Everything depends in this connection on the word which the English translators across the centuries have with almost complete unanimity rendered as "serpent."

Now the Greek word ὄφις to which the translation "serpent" responds had many associations for the inhabitants of the ancient world. It was applicable to the imaginary monsters of the starry heavens (the celestial *draco*), to the mythological powers of the primordial deep and to their offspring (the anguipeds), to the Lernaean Hydra of the Hercules stories (a special type of ὄφις) and to various chthonic powers like the οἰκουρὸς ὄφις that was supposed to live under the acropolis at Athens.[2] The translation of ὄφις by "serpent" in the rendering of Matthew is therefore thoroughly justifiable, not only because it paves the way for the statement, "If you, then, being evil . . . ," but also because it responds to the associations of the Greek word. But of course the original saying of Jesus was actually spoken in Aramaic, no doubt with the use of the word *naḥaš*, and so for the interpreter the potential connotation of what the father might have offered instead of a "fish" is not limited to what is suggested by the Greek ὄφις. One turns naturally in this connection to the biblical, Old Testament, associations of the word *naḥaš*, which are too familiar to develop in detail, but these provide no hand-hold for a different understanding of the logion since they, too, emphasize the poisonous and harmful character of the animal, and very properly so.[3] What is needed in the present context to supplement the biblical, desert-oriented connotation of the snake is

[2] See in general the article by Hartman in *P-W*, *s.v.* "Schlange."

[3] On the poisonous character of the snake see, e.g., Deut. 32:24 and Job 20:16. Less typical is the "subtleness" of the snake in Gen. 3:1 and more so the "fiery" nature of the noxious serpents in Num. 21:6 and Deut. 8:15.

something that would reflect its association with the simple domestic environment of the agricultural villages.

The kind of association required to unify the rhetorical questions of the Matthean saying at a possible earlier level of transmission can be illustrated from an analogous but quite unrelated Roman conception. This conception will be familiar to anyone who has wandered in and among the streets and houses of Herculaneum and Pompeii and has seen there in the *lararia* and on household altars representations of large green snakes. These represent the "genius" of the family and are associated with the cult of the ancestors in Roman religious thought and observance.[4] It would be utterly improper to project into the Palestine of Jesus' day any conception associating the snake with the "genius" of the family. In Jewish Palestine the family cohered by tradition in one of the twelve "tribes" and the "tribes" in the Chosen People, the nation. But it would be interesting to know whether in the agricultural villages of New Testament Palestine there existed anything comparable to what developed in connection with the ancestor cult in Italy, namely the tendency to regard a harmless garden-snake or grass-snake as something of a household pet, or at least as a welcome part of the domestic scene.

The presumption that such a conception may have existed apart from the ancestor cult in the ancient Near East is perhaps given likelihood by consideration of the story we have about the founding of Alexandria in Egypt. The story is that when Alexander the Great was outlining the site for the city he proposed to found on the Nile Delta, a snake appeared and its appearance was regarded as a favorable omen.[5] Far from being a noxious creature, the snake appears in this context as a friendly animal. It became in fact the "Good Spirit" of the city and had in the later city a sacred precinct of its own, the *temenos* of the Agathodaimon.[6]

For Palestine it seems possible to go still farther with the help of a passage in the Midrash Rabbah to Genesis 21:22 in which a folk-tale is recounted in support of the belief that snakes have a liking for the vegetable leek. The story says that a snake once came into a house from the mountains and found a bowl of leek there. It ate of the leek and after eating spat into the bowl. Being a mountain snake it was poisonous and if the people of the household had eaten of what remained of the leek they would have been poisoned by the

[4] On the snake as the "genius" of the family see G. Wissowa, *Religion und Kultus der Römer*, 2nd ed. (Munich, 1912), pp. 175 ff.
[5] For the basic version of the story see Arrian, *Anabasis* iii. 1. 5; 2. 1.
[6] On the snake as Agathodaimon see the article of Wernicke in *P-W*, *s.v.*

venom the snake had spat into the bowl. But another snake, living in the house, saw the mountain snake enter the premises. It was not able to resist the entry of the poisonous snake and thus could not prevent it from poisoning what remained of the leek. So it waited until the mountain snake had gone and then filled the bowl with dirt. Why it did this the reader of the story has to infer, but obviously the smaller snake, already in the house, was doing what it could to mitigate the danger to the inhabitants. When the members of the household found the bowl full of dirt they would naturally wash the leek and thus escape the danger of being poisoned. So the story quite by accident gives us a picture of a simple domestic situation where a little, non-poisonous snake lives in a house and where it is sufficiently a member of the household to wish to protect the other members from the harmful designs of a poisonous mountain snake that does not belong there.

We have wandered far afield from the saying of Jesus, but this is precisely what the New Testament interpreter must do to gain new insights into his material and to get beyond the "old chestnuts" of learned commentaries. Coming back now to the two rhetorical questions in the Matthean version of the saying "Seek, and you will find," we can suggest for an earlier version of the logion an interpretation of the possible offer of a "snake" in place of a "fish" that avoids the noxious implications of the "serpent" and permits us to construct a consistent image of what the father might do. What he might do, but does not, is to respond to the query of his son by giving a "stone" in place of a "loaf" and by giving a harmless "house-snake" in place of a "fish." Both of the objects are germane to the setting, for both exist in the courtyard of the simple village house. Both have verisimilitude, since the flat stepping stone of the courtyard is roughly like the flat loaf of bread, while the little house-snake has all the natural wiggliness of the fish. And the image of what the father might be also has propriety. Far from being an unnatural, inhuman being, he is the hard-hearted disaffected type who, while recognizing his son's right to expect something from him, disposes of the request by offering him the next-best, useless, shoddy substitute. The whole picture, therefore, of the choice of the substitutes that are right at hand, of the outward similarity between the substitute and the things asked for and of the callousness of the disaffected father, is in keeping with the potential tenor, the temper and the horizon of life in an agricultural village, thus continuing within the frame of the vignette painted by the saying. In contrast to the disaffected father, the typical father, also recognizing the right of the son to support, gives willingly what the young man asks for. As he provides for the essential needs of his son, so also does God provide for the essential needs of his children. How the Lucan version of the saying may have developed is not difficult to infer if we take the proposed interpretation of the core as a starting point. It was the rhetorical question suggesting the gift of a "snake" in place of a "fish" that brought about the change. Once the saying left the village environment in which the house-snake and the flat stone of the courtyard were familiar parts of the scene, and particularly when Aramaic *naḥaš* was replaced by Greek ὄφις, new overtones were sensed in what was now a reference to a "serpent." Being inconsistent with the gift of a "serpent," the question about the gift of a "stone" was dropped and replaced by one substituting a "scorpion" for an "egg." By this means the imagery of the saying was reunified. That in this connection the imaginary father of the rhetorical questions became a villain and a monster did not disturb the third Evangelist and his generation. To those using the saying of Jesus for moralizing purposes the sharpest possible contrasts between black and white and good and evil probably seemed much more effective than the gentler nuances gained from a close observation of reality.

As to the concluding statement of the saying, which is rendered in almost identical fashion by Matthew and Luke and which must therefore have stood in the Second Source, it can well have formed part of the core of the saying, save for the clause referring to "ye, who are evil." Some such conclusion was necessary, and the argument from the lesser to the greater which it uses is typical of the rhetoric both of Jesus and of his environment. The descriptive clause "ye who are evil" reflects the same moralizing outlook upon the tradition that we have found in the villainous father of the rhetorical questions in the Lucan version, only the effect in Matthew and the Second Source is less far-reaching. The entrance of such modifying factors into even the earliest documentary versions of the tradition is not surprising. No tradition is ever transmitted in a vacuum, and given the perspectives and problems of the first and second generations of Christians the adaptation of the sayings of Jesus to the promotion of Christian morality is not only the most obvious but also the easiest to discount. At the same time the necessary continuous interplay between the tradition that is being transmitted and the needs of the transmitting communities provides the justification for the effort to recreate the hypothetical core of such a saying as that under discussion here. The only proviso is that the recreation shall be in accord with the historical and factual circumstances under which it could have been spoken and to which it could have addressed itself. It is in this connection that a knowledge of the world of Jesus' day becomes important, as for instance in the bearing of the agricultural village of Palestine upon the saying "Seek, and you will find."

IV | *Rodney Branton*
COLGATE-ROCHESTER
DIVINITY SCHOOL

RESURRECTION IN THE EARLY CHURCH

Any student of the New Testament sees at once that the Resurrection is so embedded in the life and preaching of the early church that without it there would have been no church and no preaching. The evidence of the Synoptic Gospels shows clearly that without the experience of the Resurrection the demoralized disciples would never have become the apostles of a gospel that swept across their world like wildfire. The Resurrection is the one adequate explanation of the Christian Church. When the group, after its shock at the crucifixion, reassembled in Jerusalem, the Resurrection was the central topic of the preaching. The sermons in Acts are built around the affirmation, "God hath raised him from the dead . . of that we are witnesses."

The entire New Testament supports this point of view. Paul states the case pointedly when he says, "If Christ has not been raised, then our preaching is in vain and your faith is in vain . . . . If Christ has not been raised, your faith is futile and you are still in your sins" (1 Cor. 15:14-17). Paul is not here defending the Resurrection nor defining it. Rather, it is assumed, and from such an assumption he argues for the resurrection of all Christians. This is a definite indication that the Resurrection of Christ is held by the Pauline churches as an accepted fact of supreme importance. The importance of the fact is further affirmed in another passage where Paul, reflecting a more primitive idea than his own, states that Jesus, who according to the flesh was a son of David, was by the Resurrection *designated* the Son of God (Rom. 1:1-4). But the Resurrection for Paul is not only of great Christological significance; it plays a great role also in the saving act of God, where it is the pivotal point. By it, man is himself raised to new life that is death-defying. "We were baptized into his death . . . our old self was crucified with him . . . so that as Christ was raised from the dead we too might walk in newness of life" (Rom. 6) and "you have been raised with Christ" (Col. 3:1). So Paul argues for three basic ideas of the Christian faith from the Resurrection : first, it is the means whereby Jesus is designated Son of God; second, it is central to God's saving act; and third, it is the assurance of man's eternal triumph over death. It then is absolutely essential to the Pauline gospel. This is also true for the remainder of the New Testament, even though the experience is not always described in the same terms, nor is it always clearly stated as a resurrection, for at times it seems to be the Ascension or the Exaltation that is emphasized as "the rising from the dead." But we are at once confronted by the importance of the Resurrection for the primitive Church. This affirmation of Paul, and the general New Testament *kerygma* go back to an historical beginning, which rests upon the experience of the primitive disciples of Jesus and which has been transmitted to us through the four Gospels, the Letters of Paul, and non-canonical writings.

Though we see the importance attached to this event, we also recognize the problems associated with it. The sources for it are removed by many years from the events they describe. They also stem from a period when the theological and Christological ideas of the Church have begun to be crystallized. Hence the historical facts are intertwined with interpretation and combined with an ever-expanding growth of legend. For a long time the Fourth Gospel has been treated as a thoroughly theological work not primarily concerned with historical detail. As a matter of fact, the Synoptic Gospels no less than the Fourth Gospel are theological documents,[1] far more concerned with the proclamation of the faith than with the statement of fact.[2] This constitutes our first great problem in the study of the Resurrection.

The second problem concerns itself with the variations in the accounts themselves, especially with the irreconcilable elements such as the geographical location of the events of Easter morning,

---

[1] C. Beach, *The Gospel of Mark* (N.Y., 1959), pp. 11-16; R. H. Lightfoot, *History and Interpretation in the Gospels* (New York, 1935), pp. 98 ff.; F. C. Grant, *The Gospels, Their Origin and Growth* (New York, 1957), p. 104, for the theological and Christological ideas of Mark; F. C. Grant, "St. Mark," *The Interpreter's Bible*, Volume VII (Nashville, 1951), pp. 629 ff.; M. S. Enslin, "The Artistry of Mark," *JBL*, LXVI (1947), pp. 385 ff.; M. Dibelius, *From Tradition to Gospel* (New York, 1935), pp. 229 f.

[2] B. Harvie Branscomb, *The Gospel of Mark* (New York, 1959), pp. xviii ff.; Branscomb places more value on the historical than the theological. H. A. Guy, *The Origin of the Gospel of Mark* (New York, 1955), pp. 54-62, affirms both the theological and historical motive in the Gospel.

and the various historical reports which bear upon the nature of the Resurrection experience. These variations are not simply minor differences which might be expected in the ordinary reporting of an event. They are hopelessly contradictory at many points. Some of the accounts report that the experience of the Resurrection occurred in Galilee while others affirm that it took place in Jerusalem. Some accounts describe the experience in highly spiritual terms while others affirm that the risen Jesus ate fish, exhibited his physical wounds, and was flesh and bones. Some accounts include an ascension, while another not only does not include it but seems to suggest its impossibility. One account suggests that the Ascension took place on the same day as the Resurrection while another says that it took place forty days later.

These and other related problems enter any serious discussion of the Resurrection as an historical event and as the cardinal affirmation of the faith of the Church. Many of these variations may be adequately explained by the purposes of the Gospel writers. They did not intend to recount history as such, they were proclaiming a faith, they were defending their theology and Christology, they were preaching for a verdict. But for a serious student, the question as to what did happen remains a challenge and demands an answer. The answer to this question will probably never be one which finds universal acceptance. Yet such must be attempted. The only evidence is to be found in the Resurrection reports themselves viewed in the light of their own world view.

There is no doubt about the priority of the Gospel of Mark since both the Gospels of Matthew and Luke make use of it. This fact, however, does not guarantee the greater value of the Resurrection accounts in Mark. Mark's account of the events following the Crucifixion is brief but clear. The disciples have fled. The three women observe where the body was laid. After the Sabbath is past, they purchase spices to anoint Jesus. They arrive at the tomb early on Sunday and find the stone rolled back from the opening of the tomb. They enter the tomb and see a young man who tells them not to be amazed, that Jesus of Nazareth has risen, that they are to inform the disciples and Peter that he was going before them to Galilee where they would see him as he had said. The women flee and, in spite of the direct command to report the news, tell no one anything for they are afraid. This account has many problems which center around the fact that no appearance in Galilee is included and, indeed, no appearance at all. The account *implies* two appearances, both of which are to take place in Galilee.[3]

Matthew, generally regarded as the second Gospel to be written,[4] has a longer account. In it the disciples who had forsaken Jesus and fled are not in Jerusalem for the appearances. The two women come early on Sunday "to see the sepulchre," and apparently are witnesses to the astonishing events. They experience the earthquake; they see the angel so as to describe him as he descended from heaven to roll back the stone. They apparently see nothing come from the tomb, for the angel gives them the message which the young man had given the three women in the Gospel of Mark—but with an omission : there is no "and to Peter." The appearance to the disciples is to take place in Galilee. But as the women, contrary to Mark's report, start from the tomb to carry out the command of the angel, the risen Jesus meets them and gives them the identical charge which had already been given them by the angel. There follows the report of the soldiers to the authorities, who had so much expected a resurrection that they placed a guard at the tomb to safeguard it against the removal of the body. The eleven disciples go to Galilee where they see the risen Jesus. However, some of the eleven are not convinced and the doubt is not resolved. The only word is one of authority which has now "been given" to Jesus, and the disciples are commanded to go into all the world making and baptizing disciples in the name of the Father, the Son, and the Holy Spirit. The closing word is very important : "And lo, I am with you always, to the close of the age."

In the Gospel of Luke there is no prophecy that the disciples will flee, and the implication is clear that they remained in Jerusalem. The women came to the tomb early on Sunday and brought spices. They found the stone rolled away and they entered the tomb, but did not find the body. As they contemplated this problem, two men in dazzling apparel stood by them, frightening them. The men assured them that they were mistaken in seeking the living among the dead : "Remember how he told you while he was still in Galilee that the Son of Man must be delivered into the hands of sinful men,

---

[3] F. C. Grant, "Studies in the Text of St. Mark," *ATR*, XX (1938), 103 ff. Grant feels that Mark 14:28 is a gloss, and while this does not completely undercut the prediction of an appearance in Galilee, it does weaken it. The absence of 14:28 from the Fayoum fragment of Mark strengthens Grant's position.

[4] But see F. C. Grant, *The Gospels, Their Origin and Growth*, pp. 119, 127, where he argues for an earlier date for Luke and a date around the turn of the century for Matthew.

and be crucified and on the third day rise." They fled from the tomb and told the eleven disciples, who regarded their report as an idle tale. The two disciples, heretofore never mentioned in the Gospel, on the road to Emmaus saw Jesus, who on the basis of Old Testament passages interpreted the suffering and glorification of the Christ. They recognized him as Jesus in the breaking of the bread. They returned to Jerusalem that very hour and reported to the disciples, who affirmed that the Lord had appeared to Simon also. Jesus then appeared to them, though the door was shut. He affirmed that he was not a spirit but had "flesh and bones," and to prove this he ate broiled fish in their presence. Again the Old Testament was interpreted as a prophecy of these events, and a commission to preach to all the nations was included. There was the promise of power from on high. He led them out as far as Bethany and was parted from them. There is no doubt that this passage is referring to the Ascension. This all happened, it would seem, on the day of the Resurrection.

The account in John 20 is closer to Luke's account. Both are in Jerusalem, both report that Jesus appeared to the disciples privately, both include physical proofs. In the Johannine account Mary went to the tomb very early while it was still dark and discovered that the stone had been rolled away. She did not investigate, but ran to report that the body of the Lord had been taken out of the tomb. Peter and the beloved disciple ran to the tomb, entered and saw the grave clothes and returned to their homes. One disciple believed. Again Mary is near the tomb weeping when the angel asks a rather useless question, since the risen Jesus himself meets her; he instructs her not to hold him, but says: "Go tell my brethren, I am ascending to my Father and your Father, to my God and your God." On the evening of that day he appeared to the disciples behind closed doors. He exhibited his physical wounds and spoke the word of peace to them, coupling it with the commission, "As the Father hath sent me, even so I send you." He breathed on them and said, "Receive the Holy Spirit. If you forgive the sins of any they are forgiven; if you retain the sins of any they are retained." Thomas was not present and did not believe the report of the other disciples. One week later he was present with the disciples behind closed doors when Jesus again appeared and exhibited his physical wounds to Thomas personally. Thomas exclaims, "My Lord and my God!" Jesus rebukes him for needing physical proof, and adds, "Blessed are those who have not seen and yet believe." This concludes the account with no ascension story and no room for Pentecost, since the Spirit has already been given. The passage in 20:17, "I am ascending," could be understood as the progressive present, and the Resurrection-Ascension might be viewed as one act and the appearances, as to Paul, directly from heaven.

Paul's account is the earliest of the written reports and contains no physical proofs nor empty tomb or ascension. The account of the Resurrection appearances in I Cor. 15:4-8 contains much that we meet in the combined accounts of the four Gospels and some distinctly new material. His list includes an appearance to Peter, also mentioned in Luke and John's appendix; to the Twelve (Eleven?) mentioned in Matthew, Luke and John, and to all the apostles who might be included in the list of the Twelve just mentioned. The list includes new material in the appearance, first, to five hundred brethren, to James, and of course, to Paul. The third day is mentioned. No locality is given for any of the experiences. It is interesting to note that Paul uses exactly the same verb to describe the appearance to the apostles and others as he does to describe his own experience of the risen Jesus. In Gal. 1:16 he mentions his "Damascus Road" experience with the words "when he was pleased to reveal his son ἐν ἐμοί," the Greek being translated by most English translators "to me" but by Luther as "in mir"; the French has "en moi" (*version Synodale*). This use of ἐν with dative has received serious discussion from the early centuries of the Christian era to the present.[5] Taken in its simplest meaning it refers to an experience of Paul himself, an inner experience. That is the meaning which will be used in this article.[6] This term as an interpretation of "He appeared unto me" clarifies the nature of the Resurrection experiences in the thinking of Paul.

The account in John 21, which is an appendix to the Gospel, is late and shows that it has undergone rather elaborate expansion somewhat in the style of the characteristic Johannine interpretation. The disciples had returned to Galilee and had obviously returned to their old profession of fishing. At least seven disciples are mentioned, two of them unnamed and with Nathaniel added to the list. Their night of fishing was fruitless, and in the morning Jesus appeared to them standing on the shore. The miracle of the one-hundred-fifty-three fish followed at his word. He prepared breakfast and when they finished eating he confronted Peter with the question

---

[5] Cf. Jerome, *Pelagius* for "to me," Chrysostom for "through me."

[6] See Raymond T. Stamm, "Exegesis to the Epistle to the Galatians," *The Interpreter's Bible*, X (Nashville and New York, 1953), 457-458; E. D. Burton, "The Epistle to the Galatians," *ICC* (New York, 1920), pp. 28-29; George S. Duncan, "The Epistle of St. Paul to the Galatians," *Moffatt New Testament Commentary* (New York, 1934), pp. 26-30.

repeated three times : "Simon son of John, do you love me more than these?,"[7] with the accompanying imperatives to feed the sheep. There follows the prediction of Peter's martyrdom and the long life of the beloved disciple. With that the Resurrection account concludes, except that the *Parousia* of Christ is emphasized indirectly. The Galilean appearance does include an experience of a group of the disciples and a special experience of Peter. In this regard its essence seems related to the Marcan prediction.

In Acts the opening verses suggest that Luke concluded the account of "all that Jesus began to do and teach *until the day when he was taken up*, after he had given commandment through the Holy Spirit to the apostles whom he had chosen." This statement suggests that there had already been an ascension which Luke 24:13 ff. implies took place on the day of the Resurrection. Although the language of Acts 1:3 ff. has been used by many interpreters to describe the content of the teaching of the risen Christ after the Resurrection and before the Ascension in Luke 24:44, it seems impossible to harmonize "that very day" in Luke with the "during forty days" of Acts. The Acts 1:3-12 account presents forty days of fellowship and proofs with an ascension. The coming (not second coming) is predicted.

From outside the New Testament the Gospel of Peter presents what might be a conflation of the traditions of the canonical Gospels with other details added. A guard had been posted at the tomb. A crowd has gathered, and a sound issued from heaven as two beings descended. The stone rolled back from the door of the tomb and the two entered. Three emerged from the tomb, one being supported by the other two. The cross followed. There came a voice from heaven : "Hast thou preached to them that sleep? From the cross came the reply : "Yes." Another being came from heaven and took his place in the tomb. The women had come to the tomb to weep, and were raising the question : "Who will roll away for us the stone . . . that we may enter and sit. . . . If we cannot do so, yet let us cast down at the door these things which we bring for a memorial of him." They came and found the tomb open and the messenger repeated much the same as in the canonical Gospels, but significantly adds : "He is risen and is departed thither whence he was sent." The women were afraid and fled. The disciples departed each to his own house and took up their nets and went to the sea.

---

[7] G. H. C. MacGregor, "The Gospel of John," *Moffatt Commentary*, p. 373; R. Bultmann, *Das Evangelium des Johannes*, 15. Auflage (Göttingen, 1957), pp. 550 ff.; W. F. Howard and A. J. Gossip, "The Gospel According to St. John," *The Interpreter's Bible*, VIII (1952), 806 ff.

Here the fragment ends, but one expects a story somewhat of the type found in John 21. The most interesting addition is that he had been raised and had *already* ascended to that place from which he had been sent, that is to heaven. It would appear to suggest that the Resurrection is in fact the Ascension, one and the same act. This might throw light on some of the questions raised by the Gospel evidence and the early preaching in Acts.

As we look at the historical evidence, we find agreement on "the third day" in Mark, Matthew, Luke, John, and Paul. All the Gospels include an empty tomb. All speak of appearances. Not all agree upon the Ascension. There are differences among the various Gospel accounts and there are problems within the Gospel accounts themselves. In Matthew there is a decided change from the report in Mark. The women who earlier in Mark had told no one, in Matthew "departed quickly with fear and joy and ran to tell his disciples," and there are internal problems in Matthew's account. The story of the appearance to the women at the tomb breaks the text violently and awkwardly. It is hard to see the purpose of the angel's word if a short distance away is the risen Jesus himself who duplicates the message. Again there is the problem of Jewish religious officials who know and are influenced by the idea of a resurrection on the third day while the intimate disciples not only do not expect it but when Jesus appears to them do not believe it. The soldiers apparently did believe it and so also the authorities. The disciples were in Galilee and the appearance took place there, but was of such a nature as to be unconvincing to "some" of them. There is no word of reassurance or proof for the doubters. There is a highly ecclesiastical commission that encompasses world-wide evangelism, liturgical baptism, and a promise to remain with them forever. This does not leave much room for an ascension or Pentecost, but it does give some hints regarding the nature of the Resurrection and the circumstances surrounding the experience.

Between the Matthean-Marcan account and the Lucan-Johannine account there are more serious differences. The first problem is that of locale. Either the disciples were in Galilee as Mark and Matthew state or they were not. If we are claiming for the Resurrection historical objectivity then we are dealing with historical evidence, and this difference is of great importance. As the evidence for locale is studied, it might be claimed that the tradition for Galilee is as difficult to defend as that for Jerusalem, and the emphasis in this instance is not upon locale but upon fact.[8] However, the

[8] Massey Shepherd, "Paul and the Resurrection Tradition," *JBL*, LXVI (1945), 227-240.

appearances in the Gospels are complicated by the fact that they are specifically assigned to certain localities. So if the appearance to the disciples happened in Jerusalem as Luke and John say, then the Marcan-Matthean tradition that places the events of Easter Sunday seventy or more miles to the North is wrong. The older assumption, which seeks to harmonize these, does not face the nature of the Matthean account as a *first* experience. This is obviously impossible.

Another problem centers in the nature of the resurrected Jesus. In Matthew, "Lo I am with you always" seems to imply a spiritual presence somewhat like Paul's indwelling Christ, beginning with the ἐν ἐμοί. In Luke the risen Jesus walks to Emmaus, breaks bread, declares that he is no spirit, has flesh and bones, eats fish and is bodily presented. Likewise, in John he commands Mary not to hold him, exhibits his wounds, and even offers Thomas the opportunity of examining them. There can be no doubt regarding the nature of the Resurrection of Christ in these accounts. Matthew does not present such a picture, but suggests something of Paul's idea that "flesh and blood" (flesh and bones) do not inherit the Kingdom of God. There is a wide gulf between our reports at this point.

Another problem centers around the empty tomb which appears in all four Gospel accounts. In Mark three women discover the tomb empty but tell no one. In Matthew two women witness the events which lead to the empty tomb and joyfully report them. In Luke three women, not the same ones as in Mark, discover the empty tomb; up to this point no one has investigated their reports. In John, Mary discovers the stone rolled away and reports the tomb as empty; Peter and the beloved disciple investigate. Matthew heightens the story by placing guards who report the Resurrection; other accounts omit this detail. Any casual reader detects glaring discrepancies between these accounts and senses the growth of legendary detail—guards, earthquakes, angels in glistening apparel, folded grave cloths, appearances—and the non-canonical accounts carry the details on to voices from heaven with answers from the cross and other embellishments for the story.

Yet the fact remains that the early preaching in Acts does not appeal to the empty tomb as the evidence for their proclamation that Jesus had been raised from the dead. The earliest sermon in broad outline is as follows : The disciples were not drunk, but were filled with the Spirit. This was the fulfillment of the prophecy of Joel regarding the last days. It had come about through the pouring out of the Spirit by Jesus of Nazareth, who was a man approved of God by the things God had done through him. Yet sinful men had crucified him, but God had raised him as the patriarch David had foretold. Death could not hold him, and he had not been left to Hades, nor did his flesh see corruption. This Jesus had God raised up and exalted to his right hand and *he*, the exalted Jesus, had "poured out the Spirit which you see and hear." He *has been made* Lord and Messiah.

Now in this passage no appeal is made to an empty tomb which could be investigated, but a strong appeal is made to the presence of the Spirit in the group. In the last analysis this is the only evidence presented. It was essentially an affirmation of faith that Jesus had not been left to the realm of the dead (Hades), but had been elevated to the right hand of God. Here he was given new status. This cannot be investigated historically nor can it be proved or disproved on any objective grounds. The only evidence is the presence of the Spirit in the group. Furthermore, the affirmation in the New Testament preaching was not ἐκ τάφου, "from the tomb"; the term of the New Testament is almost universally ἐκ νεκρῶν, "from among the dead." If the emphasis were to be placed, as the Gospels eventually did, upon an empty tomb, then the prevailing term would have been "from the tomb" and not "from among the dead." The fact that ἐκ νεκρῶν occurs twenty-eight times in the New Testament of the Resurrection of Jesus while ἐκ τάφου does not occur even once is powerful evidence. The word τάφος is used of the tomb in the Gospels and would be expected to recur in the early preaching. It does not reappear in connection with the Resurrection faith. The early preaching in Acts and Paul's letters does not make use of any appeal to other physical manifestations such as eating fish, being flesh and bones, exhibiting wounds.

The Ascension constitutes another problem. In Matthew there is the promise of the presence with them of the "risen" Jesus always to the end of the age. This idea stands over against Luke where, on the day of the Resurrection, Jesus led the disciples out as far as Bethany and lifted his hands, blessed them, and was parted from them. This is the Ascension. In Acts the appearances continue for forty days and then he ascends into heaven, from whence he will come as he went. There was an interim between the Resurrection and the Ascension, and in the Gospels of Luke and John this is a period of physical manifestation. But generally outside the Gospels the emphasis moved quickly from the Cross to the Exaltation in heaven. Paul's statement in Phil. 2:8-9 is illustrative of this approach, which is very much like the preaching in Acts. "He became obedient unto death, even the death on the cross. Therefore God *has highly exalted him, and bestowed on him* the name which is above every name." Heb. 10:12 states that "When Christ had offered for all time a single sacrifice for sins, he sat down at the right hand of God." As a matter of fact Hebrews is strangely quiet on the Resurrection except in 13:20, which is the benediction. So also are the Johannine Epistles silent about the physical aspects of the Resurrection which could have functioned powerfully in combating the heresy invading the Church. The Cross and Exaltation of the Christ are emphasized beginning in Acts and continuing. No interim details clutter up the proclamation. He was crucified. He was exalted. This lies behind the statement in Matt. 28:16, "All authority has been given me," and in the Gospel of Peter, "He has risen and returned to the place whence he came." The Resurrection was the Ascension. But better, the Resurrection was the Exaltation.

The Resurrection is cast in the same setting as the total ministry of Jesus. The eschatological hopes of the people had been aroused by the terrible conditions through which they were passing. Many apocalyptic figures and writings appeared during this period holding out to suffering, disheartened people the hope that God was about to act through a messiah. The message of Jesus is to be understood in precisely this atmosphere. [9] There is every evidence that the disciples and at least some of the people regarded him in a messianic sense. At Caesarea Philippi the disciples were shocked by the stern command of Jesus not to proclaim him as Messiah, and by his amazing acceptance of the role of suffering. However, as Jesus and the small inner circle of disciples moved toward Jerusalem, they revealed again and again their definite messianic hopes. Up to the very end they entertained the conviction that Jesus was the Messiah. There is every reason to believe that Jesus had used the term Son of Man frequently and in an eschatological sense. He proclaimed the love and the judgment of God as he called people to repentance in view of the imminent coming of the Son of Man. This made a great impression on his hearers who understood him to say that the Son of Man would come before some of them tasted death or before the Twelve had gone through all the towns of Israel.

With such ideas and hopes the disciples were unprepared for the events of Good Friday. The Crucifixion came as a terrible and really as an impossible end to his great life and ministry and as a scandal to their eschatological and messianic hopes. Back in Galilee, demoralized by the frustrations of Passion week, they again found

---

[9] R. Bultmann, *Theology of the New Testament*, trans. by Kendrick Grobel (New York, 1951), Vol. I, pp. 17 f.

themselves where they had heard his words and felt the impact of his life. They were thinking again in Jewish apocalyptic terms and found in the picture of the heavenly Son of Man an idea that opened a whole new world to them. Jesus, while not the Christ during his early life, now had been elevated to the right hand of God where he had been given the status of Messiah,[10] and so all authority had been given to him and in his name the eschatological hopes would still be realized. A *parousia*[11] was inevitable to complete the picture, but this involved a tremendous leap of faith, for he had been crucified and buried. Yet the "eyes of faith" saw that he had not been surrendered to the realm of the dead but had come forth from this realm ἐκ νεκρῶν, and had not just survived as men in general, hoping to go in triumph on the great eschatological day from the realm of the dead to the realm of God, βασιλεία τοῦ Θεοῦ. No, Jesus had already been raised from the dead; more than that, he had been exalted to the right hand of God to a place of honor. Still more, he had been given a name above every name, Messiah. He had been designated as the heavenly Messiah and had been given all authority in heaven and in earth. In his name repentance, forgiveness and the receiving of the Spirit were proclaimed. The *Parousia* was the coming of this heavenly Messiah.

Thus the early church was the eschatological community.[12] The disciples sensed the power of the Spirit working in them. This experience of power they at first explained as the work of the risen, exalted Jesus who had been made Messiah. "Being exalted at the right hand of God, and having received from the Father the promise of the Holy Spirit, he has poured out this which you see and hear" (Acts 2:33). This was the first explanation of the relationship between Jesus and the Spirit. The group had returned from Galilee to Jerusalem where they expected the great eschatological event to be consummated. They lived in vivid expectation of the *eschaton*. Acts even includes a question, "Lord will you at this time restore the Kingdom to Israel?" This reveals the crudely nationalistic eschatological hopes of the Jerusalem group. They were sure that the exalted Jesus Messiah who had poured out the Spirit upon them would return soon, to bring the great hopes to fruition. But as time went on they changed this idea of Jesus' bestowing of the Spirit and began to identify the Spirit which they experienced *as* the Risen

[10] Felix Gils, *Jésus prophète d' après les évangiles synoptiques* (Louvain, 1959), pp. 142-153.

[11] R. Bultmann, *op. cit.*, pp. 28 ff. παρουσία never meant for Jesus a return but merely "arrival" or "advent" of the Messiah.

[12] R. Bultmann, "What Alienates Modern Man from Christianity?," *The Colgate Rochester Divinity School Bulletin*, XXXI (May, 1959), 25 f.

Christ. Paul in II Cor. 3:17 can say "The Lord (Jesus Christ) is the Spirit." This is also Matthew's meaning, "Lo I am with you always, even to the end of the age." The earliest experience was the primitive idea of Jesus exalted and given the new status of Messiah who poured out the Spirit; then the idea began to identify the Spirit[13] with the historical Jesus whom they had known. This identification is clear in the letters of Paul where the Spirit, the Spirit of God, the Spirit of Christ and the indwelling-Christ are used in consecutive passages, obviously referring to the same experience. But alongside this there grew up the more material-physical interpretations of the "rising from among the dead," changing it to "rising from the tomb." This gave rise to other convincing stories of his triumph over the grave. The accounts of the empty tomb with all the embellishments of angels, Ascension and other details are secondary growth. The events described in the Resurrection narratives must be viewed as a growth of hagiographic detail to clothe the faith that the Lord Jesus lived at God's right hand. They represent the understanding of the Resurrection held by people removed by a generation or more from the original experience. The appearances were probably "visions" which grew out of the faith that the Lord Jesus had been exalted to God's right hand. The faith produced the visions; the visions did not produce the faith.

This is why Acts proclaims the faith and does not emphasize the visions. It seems reasonable to assume that the sermons in Acts did not use the vivid Resurrection stories of the Gospels because they had not yet been produced. For the preachers in Acts, there seems to have been no lapse of time between Resurrection and Ascension, so that the better sequence would be Cross to Exaltation. Thus there is no need to try to harmonize the Galilean and Jerusalem traditions, the number of women at the tomb, the number of angels, the Ascension on Easter Sunday or forty days later and other details. These appeared as devout legends, apologetic arguments or preaching illustration. The Resurrection itself was not an event concerned with open tombs, fish-eating or even ascensions. It was a faith; and this faith was originally moulded in Jewish eschatological messianic terms which later in the Hellenistic church became a universal faith. This then, is a faith which the historian cannot prove or disprove. But the historian can study the reports and interpretations of it which make claims of an objective, historical nature.

---

[13] John Knox, *The Death of Christ* (New York 1958), p. 109, makes the realization of the identity of the Spirit with the remembered one the realization of the Resurrection.

V | *Frederick C. Grant*
UNION THEOLOGICAL
SEMINARY

THE HISTORICAL
PAUL

One of the finest sonnets in English literature begins

> Milton, thou should'st be living at this hour!
> England hath need of thee.

So wrote William Wordsworth in London in 1802. How often in the past men have cried out for the return of great leaders, great teachers, great rulers, and great thinkers, to face present crises and solve deeply involved present problems! For several generations men believed that Frederick Barbarossa was asleep in a quiet cave and would return when Europe's need became most dire. Even the emperor Nero had those who longed for his return, as in the days of "Vespasian's brutal son," the emperor Domitian, who

> Clear'd Rome of what most sham'd him.

The popular dream of *Nero redivivus* is reflected in the New Testament, in the Apocalypse of John (see Rev. 13:3; 17:8). Elsewhere in the New Testament we hear an echo of popular beliefs in Galilee that "one of the old prophets" had risen, that Jesus—or perhaps John—was Elijah come back to life again or risen from the dead, or that he was Jeremiah come again. The *Elias redivivus* hope has had a very long history, starting with the last verses of the prophet Malachi (4:5 f.), if not earlier, and surviving to this day in popular folklore, e.g., in Poland, where every Jewish child is taught to look for the coming of the prophet Elijah. Even the Messianic hope, the expectation of a return of King David or of his son or the rise of a king descended from David to liberate and rule the people of God—this also belongs in the category we are considering.

Why is this? Why do people crave the return of great men from the past? Why is the world so completely conditioned to its own past that future deliverers must really be ancient ones come back to life or returned to earth, to repeat their heroic deeds or to voice their wise counsels and so win freedom and safety for their people? I do not know the answer—the question belongs in the field of social psychology, I suppose—and it requires an answer which is something more than a catalogue of instances or a description of the religio-socio-psychological phenomenon. Certainly it is a genuine and widely spread human phenomenon; witness the efforts made during the past seventy-five years to go back to the "historical" Paul, as also to the "historical" Jesus.

At first glance, one cannot help questioning what St. Paul's contribution would be. We might appropriately quote further from Wordsworth's sonnet:

> Thy soul was like a Star, and dwelt apart:
> Thou hadst a voice whose sound was like the sea,
> Pure as the naked heavens, majestic, free—

but that is all; the rest of the poem does not apply to Paul. He did *not* "travel on life's common way in cheerful godliness" or lay upon himself "the lowliest duties"; instead, he was aflame with a transcendent apocalyptic dream, to which he gave his whole attention, thought, zeal, devotion—and eventually life itself, when he died a martyr at Rome in the year 62 or 64. His whole aim was "to become all things to all men," that he "might gain some." His missionary career carried him from Jerusalem, Damascus and Antioch to Cyprus and the heart of Anatolia, to the great cities about the Aegean Sea—Troas, Thessalonica, Philippi, Athens, Corinth, Ephesus—and finally "round about as far as Illyricum," after which he hoped to see Rome and then visit Spain. He thought of himself as the "apostle to the Gentiles"—Peter and the others were apostles to the Jews, to the Semitic world, and to the East; but Paul had been "sent forth far hence among the Gentiles," including even the wild barbarians of the far West. His life involved great endurance of "afflictions, hardship, calamities, beatings, imprisonments, tumults, labors, watching, hunger . . . in honor and dishonor, in ill repute and good repute . . . treated as an imposter, and yet . . . true; as unknown, and yet well known; as dying, and behold we live; as punished, and yet not killed; as sorrowful, yet always rejoicing; as poor, yet making many rich; as having nothing, and yet possessing everything" (II Cor. 6:4-10). Clearly a man of this high caliber, a man of limitless energy, patience, and determination, who never admitted defeat, and was struck down only to rise and push forward once more—such a man would make his mark in any generation and contribute to the shaping of its thought and to that of the generations that followed. But what would this mark be? And what was his contribution to the solution of our problems? Was he anything more than a shouting evangelist—the kind that won Emerson's cool reply "The world is coming to an end. Very well, I can do without it!"

For many long centuries Paul was viewed as a theologian; before that, for several long centuries, as only an amanuensis of the Holy Spirit, who wrote down oracular words which could be lifted out of their setting (in the context of his epistles), arranged in a more logical pattern of sacred dicta and thus form a system of dogma or a dogmatic theology. Paul was treated by Christian thinkers and writers in the same way that Plato and Homer had been expounded by their interpreters—Maximus of Tyre could quote a line of Plato or Homer to settle almost any question of politics or ethics, while others cited Homer in the interest of geography and anthropology. It is almost within our own memory that Paul has come to be viewed, interpreted, and understood as a man. Among modern interpreters of Paul, no one has contributed more than Adolf Deissmann, the father of biblical papyrology. He began his famous book on Paul—he refused to say "St." Paul, but insisted upon removing the halo—by describing him vividly as a teacher browned by the Anatolian sun, a living man, a religious devotee and propagandist under the early Roman empire: "*Ein Anatolischer und antiker Paulus, ein* homo novus *aus der Masse der Vielen und Kleinen herauswächst.*"

We have no quarrel with those who would study Paul's theological significance and who find in his thought the roots of later systems— Augustine's, Luther's, Calvin's; but we wish first of all to view him as a *man*, as Deissmann did, and then ask, not what he contributed to the fourth century or the sixteenth but what he can contribute to the twentieth. In a way, this is no novel procedure; Paul has been repeatedly rediscovered, from Marcion to Adolf Deissmann. When in the year 1496 John Colet returned from Italy, where he had learned Greek and had associated with Platonists and humanists, he began lecturing at Oxford on St. Paul, whose letters, he insisted, were to be read as one would read those of Cicero. That was surely the proper approach : if they turn out to be different from Cicero's and to contain something of deeper import, that is the joyful discovery of the reader, who finds for himself what religious inspiration and spiritual insight really mean. But to take Paul as a book of riddles or of obscure oracles, each set off as a verse by itself—as in most old-fashioned Bibles—this only leads to ever deeper obscurity, from which a system of theology may emerge but not a living man, certainly not the "new man in Christ" he thought himself to be.

There are several misconceptions that must be cleared away if we are to gain a true picture of the great apostle and his work. (1) One is the idea that he was a "rabbi" and—closely allied with this false view—another is that he owed his allegorism to his rabbinic training. He may in fact have sat at the feet of Gamaliel I (Acts 22:3), but that did not make him a rabbi. It is probable that his studies in Jerusalem were like Josephus's studies of Pharisaism (*Vita* 2), brief and superficial. The whole outlook of Paul is non-scribal, non-traditional. The men who have been really schooled in a great religious tradition and then have left it have invariably borne its stamp all their days—men like Ernest Renan or Alfred Loisy, who left French Catholicism, or John Henry Newman or Ronald Knox, who left Anglicanism. But Paul bore no traces of Tannaite methodology in his later years. Furthermore, the title "rabbi" was probably not commonly used before the Fall of Jerusalem and Jochanan ben Zakkai's reorganization of the Jewish schools.[1] Finally, it is not true that allegorism characterized rabbinic exegesis. On the contrary, literalism was the rule, and only after the literal meaning had been established were deeper meanings, parallel usages, and the systematic arrangement of ideas drawn from various parts of Scripture. Allegorism flourished in the Diaspora (*teste* Philo), not in Palestine. Those who credit Paul's allegory of Hagar and Mt. Sinai (Gal. 4:25) to his "rabbinic" education are hard pressed to find parallels in Palestinian tradition.

(2) Another misconception is the idea that Paul was a systematic theologian, who bore within the depths of his mind a vast logical

---

[1] The title is often used inaccurately by Christians. (*a*) In the time of St. Paul and of Jesus, the teachers of Israel were known as "scribes," i.e. *sopherim*, writers, book-men, copyists. As the copyists of the sacred writings, chiefly the Torah or "Law," they were most familiar with it and were therefore qualified to be its accredited expounders or teachers. (See the description of the ideal scribe in Sirach 39, and George Foot Moore's exposition in *Judaism*, Vol. I, pp. 308-22.) (*b*) The Pharisees were a society, a "brotherhood," of laymen who undertook to live in accordance with the scribal exposition of man's duty under the divine Covenant. They were "Separatists" who avoided all contact with idolatry and idolaters and devoted themselves to the complete and perfect observance of "the Law's demands." They were not teachers, though a scribe might be—and often was—a member of their society. (*c*) The "rabbis" were the scribal teachers of Israel, usually Pharisaic in outlook and aim, who strove to keep the nation loyal to God and his revelation in spite of the disastrous and disillusioning outcome of the war in A.D. 66-70. "Rabbi" means "my teacher" or "my master"—a title of respect and even reverence for a devoted spiritual guide and moral counsellor (something like a "spiritual director" in Christian practice).

structure of theology, only gradually unfolding it in his Epistles. But this is only a sixteenth-seventeenth century delusion—it is really an old Protestant dogmatic theologian looking down a well and identifying his own reflection with the face of Paul. Paul was a missionary, a devotee, an enthusiast, a mystic, a poet—and anyone for whom these terms are either incomprehensible or repellent had better let Paul alone. He had far more in common with St. Francis of Assisi or with Francis Xavier than with St. Thomas Aquinas; far more with Aristides the second century sophist or the Hermetic writers than with Theon of Smyrna or the authors of systematic textbooks of philosophy in the second, third or fourth century. To expound a "theology" of Paul is like expounding a "theology" of Isaiah or the Koran, where ideas burn like flares that light the whole sky, instead of as a firm and constant pattern of stars in astronomical symmetry.

(3) Another misconception of Paul is related to this one : he is credited with creating a logical system of theology, independently of the Bible; but his own deepest interest was in understanding and interpreting the Old Testament. Certainly, for him, all "theology" was "biblical theology," and he now possessed, so he believed, the key to a full and final disclosure of the meaning of Scripture, its "mysteries," the divine secret "hid from ages and generations" but at last made known through Christian prophets and evangelists. For Paul, *Christ* was the key to the Old Testament, the goal and center of divine revelation. This was of course a type of mysticism— not "nature-mysticism" nor "God-mysticism," both of which were familiar to the ancient world, but "Christ-mysticism" plus "Scripture-mysticism," something new in the world at that time but common enough in later periods of Christian history, thanks to Paul and those whom he influenced.

Fifty years ago it was commonly supposed that Paul derived much of his inspiration and many of his ideas from the Stoics. The theory has steadily crumbled under the stress of modern research. True, he used a few Stoic terms, but so did everyone else. Even these terms were not the ones chosen as evidence fifty years ago : συνείδησις, for example, the Greek word for "conscience." This was not "a Stoic commonplace," as we used to think, but is found in many Hellenistic writers after Menander, in papyri and inscriptions, in Jewish as well as Greek writers, *and also* in the Stoics.

The quarry from which Paul drew his ideas and his terms was really the Greek Bible, the Septuagint—not the Hebrew Bible, which he probably did not often use. His exegesis was not that of the schools, either the Palestinian or the Alexandrian, but his own.

This was often forced, sometimes fantastic, always unique—like the exegesis of others in his own time and also like that of far later students of Holy Writ, who have found whatever they looked for in its pages. Anyone reading the Bible in complete isolation, with only his own methods and presuppositions to guide him but with a profound sense of the inspiration of Scripture, is likely to come up with new ideas and interpretations, with which he then proceeds to challenge the recognized religious authorities. This has happened hundreds of times in the course of religious history. Paul's results were often superior to those of his contemporaries, both Philo the allegorist and the strict traditionists of Palestine. But these results were not due to a more profound or truer understanding of the Scripture; they were due to the intuitions of a religious genius, inspired by a conception of the meaning of God's revelation, his purposes which were now finally realized in Christ, and of the contemporary eschatological winding-up of all human history. Paul really *did* find true things in the Bible, which really *had* been "hid from ages and generations" and were still hid from the eyes of both strict legalists and fancy-guided allegorists. Above all, his profound ethical instinct, which was as deep and real as this same Jewish trait found in Philo and the Tannaim, led him to the "deep things of God" as they were revealed—or partly revealed and partly veiled—in Holy Scripture.

(4) Still another misinterpretation of Paul stands in the way of a clear conception of his mind, his personality, and his purposes: it is the assumption that he completely rejected and repudiated his Jewish religious inheritance. But he himself denied this, in vehement terms. When Jewish opponents attacked him and denied his apostolic authority on the ground that he was a non-Jewish upstart, he replied: "Are they Hebrews? So am I. Are they Israelites? So am I. Are they descendants of Abraham? So am I. Are they servants of Christ? I am a better one—I am talking like a madman—with far greater labors, far more imprisonments, with countless beatings, and often near death" (II Cor. 11:22-23). In another letter he insisted that he was a member of "the people of Israel, of the tribe of Benjamin, a Hebrew born of Hebrews [i.e., a born Jew], as to the Law a Pharisee, . . . as to righteousness under the Law, blameless" (Phil. 3:5 f.; cf. Acts 23:6). It was his deepest conviction that the Church, far from being a Gentile organization or even a severed branch of Judaism, was the true, authentic "Israel of God," the "new Israel" which was the "true Israel," the authentic continuation of the ancient line of divine revelation and human response and hence the heir to all the promises of God. This was of course the

natural viewpoint of the reformer and has parallels everywhere in the history of religion, wherever in fact a new and revolutionary movement has endeavored to take over a traditional faith, and, failing to do so, has gone its separate way. There are many illustrations of this principle to be found in America, with its multitude of sects and subdivisions of sects.

The sincerity and the seriousness of Paul's view led him not to reject and condemn his ancestral faith—he was no convert from paganism who "now destroyed what once he had adored, and now adored what once he had destroyed"—but to view with the most utter pain, distress, and grief the self-condemnation and rejection (as he viewed it) of the great body of the Jewish people who had failed to accept the proclamation of Jesus as the promised Messiah. The intellectual and emotional agony which this fact caused Paul is written large in chapters 9-11 of his Epistle to the Romans : "I am speaking the truth in Christ, I am not lying; my conscience bears me witness in the Holy Spirit, that I have great sorrow and unceasing anguish in my heart. For I could wish that I myself were accursed and cut off from Christ for the sake of my brethren, my kinsmen by race. They are Israelites, and to them *belong* the sonship, the glory, the covenants, the giving of the Law, the worship, and the promises; to them belong the patriarchs, and of their race, according to the flesh [i.e., by physical descent], is the Christ. [May] God, who is over all, be blessed for ever! Amen" (Rom. 9:1-5). He solves his frustrating problem by falling back upon the promise (which is still cited in the Jewish Prayer Book), "All Israel will be saved" (Rom. 11:26; *cf.* "All Israel has a part in the life to come"). And he concludes that it has been by the mysterious yet sublime act of God himself that some Israelites have been blinded temporarily to the glory of the final revelation, so that the Gentiles (he is writing to Gentiles, 11:13) may enter and inherit the promise; and then, eventually, the remainder of the Jews will be received and made partakers of eternal life. That is Paul's "philosophy of history," his solution of the failure of Israel as a whole to accept and respond to the gospel. The Jewish "rejection" of Christ (as he views it) was not only foreseen but also fore-ordained by God and is a part of the divine "plan of the ages" by which God is bringing to pass his final purposes of good for all mankind. For it is the salvation of all men everywhere that God has in mind and has had in mind from the beginning. The very language of the ancient promise makes this clear : "In thee [Abraham], shall *all* the nations be blessed" (Gal. 3:8).[2]

---

[2] See also "Paul the Pharisee," the Mary Fitch Page Lecture for 1960 at the

Now that we have removed some of the modern misunderstandings of Paul, we are in a better position to answer our question, What has he to contribute to the solution of our modern problems?

(1) In the first place, he was an implacable opponent of racism, discrimination and intolerance. The Christian, he maintained, was a "new man in Christ"—he had "died" and his life was "hid with Christ in God" (Col. 3:3). This, as I have indicated, was a new type of mysticism, "Christ-mysticism" or "personal mysticism" we may call it, not found in either Judaism or Greco-Roman religion in the first century, though there were to be approaches to it in the second century in the cults of Isis and Asclepius. And it had an intensely practical application. The "new man in Christ" was *really* new, not just a converted Anatolian or Syrian or Italian : "Here there cannot be Greek and Jew, circumcised and uncircumcised, barbarian, Scythian, slave, freeman, but Christ is all, and in all" (Col. 3:11). Certain people who today mask as Christians, and extremely conservative ones at that, would find short shrift at Paul's hands when he discovered that they were spreading the poison of race-hatred and intolerance.

(2) He was opposed to fanaticism. The fruits of the Spirit, i.e., of direct inspiration by the Holy Spirit, were not *glossolalia* or "speaking with tongues" but "love, joy, peace, patience, kindness, goodness, faithfulness, gentleness, self-control. . . . And those who belong to Christ have crucified the flesh with its passions and lusts" (Gal. 5:22-24). And he adds, "If we live by the Spirit, let us also walk by the Spirit" (vs. 25). Life in the Spirit is no occasional possession, by us—or rapture, in which we yield ourselves—but a steady self-discipline in the way of righteousness.

(3) He was a courageous and determined leader who did not hesitate to stand out in the open, without fear or favor, and take the issues of the time in both hands, demanding and compelling a solution of their intolerable problems. He solved the difficulty which confronts every religion sooner or later, and many times over —when it becomes old enough—viz., how to revise its own standards, reform its own doctrines, edit its own sacred books, abandon out-moded positions and theories, and rise to new heights of spiritual insight and respond to new calls of duty. For example, the observance of the ceremonial law was becoming purely formal and local; Judaism had spread everywhere in East and West, and the sacrificial cult in Jerusalem was impossible of observance for most

Berkeley Divinity School in New Haven; it forms the substance of Ch. VII in my book, *Roman Hellenism and the New Testament* (Edinburgh and New York, 1961).

Jews, not only three times a year but any time—even once in a lifetime for some persons. Obviously the traditional cult was tied to the past, "growing old" and "ready to vanish away," as the author of the homily known as the Letter to Hebrews (8:13) said of the sacrificial worship. Obviously prayer, study, the practice of religion could go on without it, as the rabbis said after the destruction of the temple in the year 70. But Paul had faced the problem in the forties and fifties, and he faced it as a Christian. The Old Testament, the sacred Jewish Scriptures, were undoubtedly inspired, but most Christians were no longer circumcised, no longer offered sacrifices in the temple at Jerusalem, and did not consistently observe the food laws. How could the two attitudes be harmonized—acceptance of divine inspiration and disregard of the explicit commands of the inspired writings? Only a man of immense genius or of unusual courage could undertake the solution of this contradiction.

(4) The solution lies in the area of his total view of the Scripture, which is far removed from the modern literalistic, bibliolatrous, "fundamentalist" view. Nor was it a purely "allegorist" interpretation of the kind the pagan writers used in getting around the scandalous tales in Homer and in the popular mythology. Paul's view is that the Scripture is inspired writing well enough, and that the writers of the Bible were inspired men, but he also recognizes the thorough humanness of both the writing and the men who wrote. Often his quotations begin λέγει or λέγει ἡ γραφή—that is, "it says" (in Scripture), or "Scripture says"—and only rarely does he imply, "God says," though the over-all divine authority of the book of books is unquestioned. But God lets human writers write for him, human speakers speak for him, and, as one of the ancient rabbis said, "The Torah speaks human language." Therefore we must not pin God down to our interpretations; he has thoughts that are far beyond our comprehension, and the obvious paradoxes and problems of Scripture are resolved on a higher level than human understanding. "O the depth of the riches and wisdom and knowledge of God! How unsearchable are his judgments and how inscrutable his ways!" (Rom. 11:33). Only the religiously minded, only the truly spiritual can grasp and interpret these deep mysteries. The plodding pedestrian who merely literalizes and thus makes more problems for himself and others has no place here. For all his disagreement with the rabbis, Paul had a thorough respect for learning. Neither the dull literalist nor the gushy sentimentalist (who doubtless claimed to "possess the Spirit") could contribute much to the real understanding of Holy Writ. This, I think, Paul would insist upon today, were he among us.

(5) Paul had a deep respect for law and order and recognized the constituted authority of the Roman Empire as divinely ordained. He was no revolutionist and shared none of the views of the Zealots, who were leading Jewish Palestine in the direction of revolt, bloodshed and eventual destruction. The whole chapter at the end of Romans (chap. 13) is a commentary on the words of Jesus, "Render to Caesar the things that are Caesar's, and to God the things that are God's (Mark 12:17)—for Jesus also was an anti-Zealot, an anti-revolutionist. Considering the views set forth by other early Christians—e.g., the author of the Apocalypse of John—the sanity and sobriety of Paul is clear and distinct. Would that *his* words had fallen on the ears of the authorities, rather than those of the fanatical minority who provoked opposition and persecution, confident that their overt acts of disloyalty would bring God to their rescue. I am sure Paul would have approved the great speech which Josephus places on the lips of King Agrippa II in Book II of his *Jewish War*.[3]

(6) Another principle of Paul's religion which has deep relevance for today is his constant insistence upon monotheism. He is not, like some modern advocates of a one-sided Christianity, a messianist or Christologist first and a theist second. He keeps the idea of God, the will of God, the nature and character of God, the purpose of God, central and primary. All things are "through Christ" but "from God." Paul would not approve the Jesuolatry of much modern preaching, which seems to be baffled and distorted by the old query : "Jesus we know, and Paul we know, but who are you "— i.e., *God* is "the unknowable," the "wholly other," the unapproachable, the inconceivable (see Acts 19:15). The flippant modern cliché, still sometimes heard in spite of a generation of "neo-orthodoxy," viz., we believe in the "Christ-like God," would be impossible on Paul's lips. He was too good a Jew—and too much a Christian—for that.

(7) Another emphasis of Paul is upon the visible Church within the larger body of society, where it must act as leaven and where Christians must let their example be seen and their influence be felt. The Church is no *ecclesiola in ecclesia;* that is a false idea, derived from the exigencies of post-Reformation apologetics and polemics, not from the New Testament. What it has led to in modern times is clear enough : e.g., the refusal of the "German Christian" minority to take a stand against Hitler until it was too late. Their excuse was that the Church has nothing to do with politics and must leave statecraft to the experts—i.e., the men who control ships and guns.

---

[3] §§ 345-401.

(8) Another point is Paul's restraint. He refuses to ride a theory or an idea to death. He now and then uses language that sounds very much like the later doctrine of original sin, or full predestination, or dualism, or gnosticism, or docetism, or encratism—and a dozen other "heresies" which took their departure from chance words found in his Epistles. But Paul did not hold these views. Again, he was too Jewish, too Christian, for that.

(9) For although he was persecuted by his former coreligionists, he insisted that he was a loyal Jew and he carried this protest with him all his life. I for one believe that the Jewish emphasis in Christianity is still important as well as valid and will make for sanity and sobriety in many areas where all is confusion, discord, and even hatred, on several levels, social as well as religious, and even political. As the late Pope Pius XII said during the persecution of the Jews in Italy, "We Christians are Jews, too.' It is Paul's catholicity of temper and outlook that is especially needed today, to offset the perversion of Christianity at the hands of the violent and bigoted, the fanatical, even diabolical haters of their fellow men.

(10) Still another trait, characteristically Jewish and at the same time basic to the New Testament, is the primacy of ethics in the religion of Paul : faith in God, whose will is righteous and who demands righteousness from men, is the faith which lies at the heart of Paul's religion. Take, for example, the great Christological passage in Philippians chapter 2. The whole motivation is ethical : "Have this mind among yourselves, which you have in Christ Jesus, who though he was in the form of God, did not count equality with God a thing to be grasped [i.e. seized, or snatched], but emptied himself, taking the form of a servant, being born in the likeness of men"—and even dying as a man, the shameful death of the cross (Phil. 2:5-8). As in the Old Testament and in Judaism, religion and ethics are simply inseparable. A non-ethical Christianity is inconceivable, as Paul understands and expounds it. This also needs emphasis today. We hear, alas, that the Sermon on the Mount is "mere ethics," and that "righteousness" is motivated by an attempt to gain credit with God, win merit, and save one's own soul. Could anything be more completely opposed to the New Testament as a whole, or to Paul in particular—not to mention the teaching of Jesus?

(11) Paul used contemporary science and even mythology to express religious insights. He was not wholly "biblical," and his preaching must have sparkled with the figures, the images, the racy idiom of the current *koine* Greek; Deissmann has noted its use in dozens of passages in Paul's letters. He was a contemporary to his

contemporaries, "all things to all men" (I Cor. 9:19-23), speaking the language of everyday conversation, not the rhetorical "efforts" of the sophists and atticists and of all merely academic minds. This also is a lesson for today. When will preachers stop using a worn-out vocabulary which no one can understand without an Elizabethan—or at least a Jacobean—glossary?

(12) He was a combination of liberal and conservative: a true liberal, for he had convictions to be liberal about; a true conservative, for he preserved and maintained ideas without flaunting them as red banners inviting opposition and destruction. He tried to persuade, not to compel belief and acceptance of the gospel. He knew and admired the gentleness, the ἐπιείκεια of Christ (II Cor. 10:1); see his marriage teaching in I Cor. 7, for example. A true liberal is not a man without convictions but one who has them, firmly implanted; but he is willing to live and let live, to let other men hold their own views on disputed points, and he insists upon maintaining charity and goodwill in spite of divergence and even debate. The one thing Paul could not stand was hypocrisy and underhandedness and the attempt to undermine an opponent by personal attack, gossip, and "running down" (as the whole Corinthian correspondence makes plain). In this also he was like Jesus, who excoriated hypocrisy but was endlessly patient with sincere misunderstanding and limited yet real goodwill.

(13) Finally, he did not allow a philosophical theology to override the religious outlook of himself or others. The "philosophy" and "vain deceit" which get equated in the New Testament were probably both of them relatively superficial—not Platonism or Aristotelianism, I am sure, but the philosophy of the chattering amateurs in the marketplace. Yet the principle is sound, and needs repeating today: philosophy, even philosophy of religion, is not religion, is not faith, is not good works, is not hope or charity or the love of God. We theologians must never forget this.

VI | *Robert M. Grant*
UNIVERSITY OF CHICAGO

HELLENISTIC
ELEMENTS IN
I CORINTHIANS

Anyone who deals seriously with the problem of Christian origins is likely to be impressed by the extent to which the gospel treasure is contained in earthen vessels—not just in jars like those of Qumran or Nag-Hammadi but in the whole setting provided by the Church's mission to the Greco-Roman world. The earliest Christian documents, the letters of the apostle Paul, clearly indicate the fact that early Christians not only proclaimed the gospel but also thought and argued about it. Indeed, when we consider such a letter as I Corinthians we cannot fail to notice that Paul is rarely content with proclamation (if there is such a thing as purely "kerygmatic" preaching); he discusses the meaning of the gospel in terms comprehensible both to himself and to his readers. He relies on authorities meaningful within the Church alone, such as Old Testament prefigurations and prophecies, the deeds and words of Jesus, his own status as an apostle, and the practices of the universal Church.[1] More than that, he appeals to the Corinthians' own understanding of life, to their human wisdom. "I speak as to sensible men; judge for yourselves what I say" (10:15); "judge for yourselves" (11:13). For this reason he uses the question "do you not know?" ten times in this letter and only once elsewhere. Most of the matters the Corinthians ought to be able to understand are derived from Christian teaching, but they are also expected to recognize that "a little yeast raises a whole lump of dough" (5:7), that priests generally eat sacrificial meats (9:13), and that only one runner in a race gets

---

[1] On Paul's authorities in I Corinthians cf. H. von Campenhausen in *Sitzungsberichte der Heidelberger Akademie der Wissenschaften*, 1957, no. 2.

the prize (9:24). In other words, Paul can build his arguments on data both Christian and non-Christian.[2] In this letter we also find terms which reflect conventional moral judgments. One of them is the word "shameful." It often takes the place of any logical or theological argument, and we are not surprised to find Paul using it once in a claim that women must not be unveiled (11:5-6); here he is upholding Semitic (and Tarsan) custom against Hellenistic practice.[3] He uses it again in denouncing women who speak in church (14:35); they did not ordinarily speak in the synagogue.[4] Anyone could use this word, but we should point out that not everyone would contrast it with πρέπον, what is suitable or fitting, both morally and esthetically (11:13). Our word "decorous" comes from the usual Latin translation of the word, which was especially popular in the Middle Stoa.[5] Again, there is the word συμφέρει, "it is beneficial," another term which Paul uses only in his letters to the Corinthians; it also occurs in Roman Stoicism. Indeed, a contrast like the one he draws in I Corinthians 6:12 and 10:23, between the Corinthians' "everything is permissible" and his own "not everything is beneficial," is also employed by his contemporary, the Roman Stoic Musonius.[6]

Perhaps the most significant terms of all are those to which both Paul and his Corinthian correspondents appeal : συνείδησις and φύσις. Συνείδησις is used in a good many senses, which have been ably analyzed by C. A. Pierce.[7] In I Corinthians Paul uses the verb σύνοιδα once (4:4) when he says, "I have nothing on my conscience," i.e., "I am not conscious of any wrong-doing for which I might be blamed." The noun occurs in passages where he is dealing with the "conscientious scruples" of the "weak" brethren who are afraid of eating sacrificial meats. The "strong" brethren to whom Paul is writing have nothing on their consciences; they do not regard eating these meats as sinful, and Paul quotes a good many of their remarks to this effect. They have γνῶσις, and a good deal of their γνῶσις consists of their συνείδησις, their "awareness" that dietary regulations do not apply to them.[8] The term συνείδησις ,as Pierce has shown, is not specifically Stoic or even philosophical; it is, however, part of

---

[2] The second example is related to the history of religion; perhaps the third is, too; cf. A. Ehrhardt in *ZNW*, XLVIII (1957), 101-110.

[3] Tertullian *De corona* 4; Dio Chrysostom *Or.* xxxiii. 48.

[4] Cf. J. Weiss, *Der erste Korintherbrief* (Göttingen, 1910), p. 342, n. 1.

[5] M. Pohlenz in *Nachrichten von der Gesellschaft der Wissenschaften zu Göttingen*, 1933, *Philol.-Hist. Kl.*, 53-92.

[6] Musonius Rufus, ed. O. Hense (Leipzig, 1905), p. 122.

[7] *Conscience in the New Testament* (Chicago, 1955).

[8] Cf. J. Dupont, *Gnosis* (Louvain, 1949), pp. 266-82.

the baggage carried by an ordinary educated Greco-Roman man. Paul apparently takes it over from the Corinthians, accepts it, and uses it himself not only here and in II Corinthians but also in Romans (three times).

Φύσις is of course a term used in Greco-Roman philosophy to denote what the author or speaker regards as "natural" and therefore morally good. Stoics and Cynics were fondest if it, but others employed it, too. Usually the difference, if any, between what was natural and what was conventional was left unexamined.[9] Now we know that the Corinthians were rather enthusiastic about arguments from "nature." "Meats for the belly, the belly for meats," they exclaimed at the beginning of their argument for the naturalness of indiscriminate sexual activity (6:13); here they followed the line of argument ascribed to the Cynic Diogenes of Corinth.[10] At that point Paul answered them with an eschatological denunciation and followed it up with an appeal based on their oneness with Christ. But when he found himself at a loss in proving that women should be veiled in church he had to appeal to the Corinthians' sense of decorum (11:13) and he had to give an argument from "nature." "Does not nature itself teach that if a man has long hair it is a disgrace for him, while if a woman has long hair it is her glory?" (11: 14-15). Here "nature" clearly means "convention," or at least it means "convention" to us. More probably, in Paul's mind there was something innately wrong about men who wore their hair long. In Romans 1:26-27 it is clear that he regarded "nature" as providing a genuine norm for moral behavior, especially in matters of sex. Of course, since it was God who had created nature, Paul did not regard "natural law" as an independent moral authority; but it was an authority for him.[11]

Beyond these matters of terminology lies the apostle's appeal to the authority of analogy and moral pronouncement. Naturally the use of analogy was not restricted to Greeks and Romans. We find it in the Old Testament, at Qumran and elsewhere, and above all in the teaching of Jesus. Indeed, we may disregard Greco-Roman parallels to the analogies of planting and watering and building on a foundation (3:5-15) because of the parallels already available in the Old Testament. But we cannot disregard the word which

---

[9] Mr. W. R. Schoedel is examining this problem in his University of Chicago dissertation.

[10] Diogenes Laertius *Lives of the Philosophers* vi. 69; Dio Chrysostom *Or.* vi. 17-20.

[11] In the Roman passage φύσις and χρῆσις, sometimes contrasted, are treated as coordinate.

Paul uses when he describes what he has done with the analogies. He says that he has been "referring matters figuratively"(μετασχηματίζειν) to himself and to Apollos for the Corinthians' sake; and the word he uses is derived from Greco-Roman rhetoric.[12] In other words, while his materials are Jewish, his method is self-consciously Greek. Four other analogies, or groups of analogies, are Greco-Roman in content. First there is the well-known analogy derived from the persons who contend in games. All run; one wins. Athletes are continent in order to win a fading crown. Athletes run a straight course and hit their opponents, not the air (9:24-27). All this is no more than an illustration for Paul's own thought. But to draw a clear line between illustrations and essential content is a harder task than one might suppose. The illustration, after all, is supposed to make the idea convincing to one's audience; it may also make it clearer to oneself.

Then there is the famous analogy of the Church as a body (12:12-27).[13] To be sure, Paul carefully explains that he is speaking about the body of Christ, into which Christians were baptized (12:13, 27). But apart from the two verses which bridge the gap between the analogy and that of which it is an analogy, there is nothing in this section which cannot be exactly paralleled in Greco-Roman literature. Paul has simply taken over the contemporary picture of the body politic as consisting of many members with different functions and has applied it to the body politic of the Church—the subject he is discussing in chapters 12-24.

Again, his analogies related to distinct speech, in I Corinthians 14—analogies which John Chrysostom called "as usual, rather far-fetched"[14]—all find their sources in the Greco-Roman world, where we encounter the ideas that, like men, musical instruments must give distinct sounds, and that failure to learn languages results in one's being regarded as a barbarian.[15]

Finally, the analogies used to prove the possibility of a resurrection body different from the mortal body are paralleled not in Jewish but in Hellenistic and Greco-Roman thought. The figure of the seed (15:36-38) was used by some rabbis to prove not the reality

---

[12] F. H. Olson in *JTS*, XVII (1915-16), 379-84.

[13] *Cf.* W. Nestle in *Klio*, XXI (1927), 350-60; W. L. Knox in *JTS*, XXXIX, (1938), 243-46.

[14] Migne, *Patrologia Graeca*, LXI, 299A (but Chrysostom means that Paul starts with more remote examples and then comes closer to his subject).

[15] Diogenes Laertius *Lives* vi. 64; Dio Chrysostom *Or.* viii. 2 (A. Oltramare, *Les origines de la diatribe romaine*, [Lausanne, 1926], p. 57, n. 1.)

of a resurrection body but the reality of a risen person's clothes.[16] The mention of different kinds of "flesh" (15:39) has Jewish coloring, but if "flesh" here means "body" the transition from what precedes to what follows is a good deal clearer, and the statement is paralleled in popular philosophy. The remarks about the varying degrees of brilliance among heavenly bodies (15:40-41) have, I think, no Jewish parallel at all, but such matters were discussed, and in much the same way, by Greeks and Romans. Finally, the term "spiritual body," toward which the discussion leads, has Peripatetic and Stoic precedents but, as far as I know, none in Judaism or in the Old Testament.[17]

In addition to the analogies there are also statements which clearly reflect conditions found in the Greco-Roman world. For one thing, when Paul criticizes the community for not expelling a man who lives with his stepmother, he claims (rather optimistically) that such cases are not found "even among the Gentiles" (5:1). In other words, at this point he feels free to use the relatively high morality (or law) of the Greco-Roman world as a lever by which to upset the Corinthians' complacency. Another example occurs when Paul tells them that it would be better to be harmed than to harm others (6:7). Obviously the statement is related to, and perhaps based upon, the teaching of Jesus, but in form it is paralleled almost exactly in Hellenistic philosophy,[18] and since Paul does not refer to Jesus at this point we may suppose that the Corinthians could recognize the moral validity of the aphorism without such a reference. Another sentence in the same chapter, "He who commits fornication sins against his own body" (6:18), is found almost word for word in Roman Stoicism.[19]

Paul's discussion of the trials of married life in I Corinthians 7 is not unlike what we find among the pessimistic authors of Jewish wisdom literature, but it is more closely paralleled in Greco-Roman writings which explain how wives and children get in the philosopher's way.[20] And while the famous passage on "having as not

---

[16] References in W. D. Davies, *Paul and Rabbinic Judaism* (London, 1948), pp. 305-6.

[17] H. Diels, *Doxographi Graeci* (Berlin, 1879), 570, line 23; H. von Arnim, *Stoicorum veterum fragmenta*, II (Leipzig, 1923), 310 and 1054.

[18] References by E. Lehmann-A. Fridrichsen in *Theologische Studien und Kritiken*, XCIV (1922), 76.

[19] Von Arnim, *op.cit.*, III, 289; Musonius Rufus, *op.cit.*, p. 65, lines 6-10. The preceding words, "Every sin a man may commit is outside the body," seem to come from Paul's opponents. Motives, not actions, are important (cf. Clement *Strom.* iii. 34. 2; Origen *Contra Celsum* iv. 26 and 45).

[20] Cf. E. Bickel, *Diatribe in Senecae philosophi fragmenta*, I (Leipzig, 1915).

having" does resemble a section in II Esdras and, like it, is eschatologically sanctioned, there are many Cynic-Stoic parallels to the form and the content of Paul's words.[21] The notion of "using one's present circumstances" in regard to being a slave (7:21) finds its best commentary in the teaching of Epictetus.[22]

The last example of the Hellenistic elements in I Corinthians we shall provide consists of Paul's panegyric on Christian love in Chapter 13. Lehmann and Fridrichsen seem to have gone too far when they spoke of this chapter as consisting of "a Christian-Stoic diatribe."[23] But did they go much too far? We should agree with those who have held that Paul's point of departure lies in the love of God expressed in Jesus, the one of whom he says, "He loved me and gave himself for me" (Gal. 2:20). But the rhetorical skill with which Paul has worked out his clauses and his sentences in this chapter is by no means spontaneous. It reflects a careful study either of rhetorical manuals or of some literary model or models. Admittedly we have no idea of what Paul's sources were.[24] It seems certain that they existed.

From the examples we have cited (and of course there are others, to be found in Bultmann's study of Paul and the diatribe-form and Weiss's great commentary on this Epistle) we can see that while he certainly became "to the Jews as a Jew" (9:20), he also became to the Greeks as a Greek. He was seeking not what would benefit him—or preserve his Christianity in its pristine purity—but what would benefit the many, so that they might be saved (10:33). In the process of this search, and of the communication of the findings, he himself achieved fuller understanding of the meaning of the gospel. Early Christians sometimes presented their community as something which was neither Jewish nor Greek but what we might call a "third force." Historically speaking, we should be inclined to substitute "both" for "neither." The Church had roots in Judaism, though sometimes modern scholars are tempted to exaggerate the depth of the roots; it came to its flowering in the Greco-Roman world. Perhaps we could say, borrowing Paul's metaphor (3:6), that Palestine planted, Hellas watered, but God gave the growth.

There is one danger which may arise when we think of Paul's thought as specifically Jewish or Hellenistic. We may tend to think of these clusters of ideas as antithetical or mutually exclusive. Such

[21] Diogenes Laertius vi. 29; Epictetus *Diss.* III.xxiv. 60; IV.i. 159.
[22] Epictetus *Diss.* IV.i. 33-40; cf. Dio Chrysostom *Or.* x.
[23] E. Lehmann-A. Fridrichsen, *op.cit.*, 55-95.
[24] Cf. Maximus of Tyre *Or.* xx. 2; A. Fridrichsen in *JTS*, XXI (1919-20), 169-71.

a notion would be historically wrong, since in the Hellenistic world and in the Roman Empire there was a great deal of intercultural communication. Paul wrote in Greek; he read the Old Testament in Greek; he usually spoke Greek. At the same time, he could think of himself (if occasion demanded) as "a Hebrew of Hebrew parents" (Phil. 3:5; cf. II Cor. 11:22; Rom. 11:1; Gal. 2:15). Sharp distinctions may or may not serve to clarify our thought, but we must beware of assuming that they correspond exactly with realities in antiquity.

VII | *Amos N. Wilder*

HARVARD DIVINITY SCHOOL

SOCIAL FACTORS IN EARLY CHRISTIAN ESCHATOLOGY

In his introduction to *The Study of the Bible Today and Tomorrow*, Harold R. Willoughby stressed an approach to biblical study which had been fostered by his own teachers and colleagues. He writes as follows :

> In the midwestern area, specifically centered in Chicago, there developed the most coherent social-history group to emerge among the biblical researchers of America. Their applications of social-historical methodology to the investigation of the environments, the literature, and the history of the early Christians have been quite extensive.[1]

This approach to the history of religions had its favoring circumstance in the vigor of the social sciences in America in the twentieth century and in the relating of sociology to history and historiography.[2] For what we have in mind is not merely the usual attention to backgrounds and life situation but a specifically sociological approach. We must limit ourselves in what follows in this paper to a redefinition of this approach in the light of earlier work and to questions of method.

It is understandable that students of the higher forms of religion have not been as disposed to recognize the sociological involvement of their material as students of primitive religion. In more developed religions doctrine, literature or piety become of interest for their own sake and are studied genetically or comparatively in abstrac-

---

[1] (Chicago, 1947), pp. xiv-xv.
[2] See "Biblical Hermeneutics and American Scholarship" in *Neutestamentliche Studien für Rudolf Bultmann* (Berlin, 1954), pp. 29-30.

tion from the life context. The case of the history of art is illuminating. The socio-economic or socio-political involvement of the graphic arts is clearest and most illuminating in the case of ancient or primitive art. When we deal with the art of western Europe in which patent tribal or civic or national determinations are absent we are not to suppose that social factors are less operative; they are only more complex. Certainly the Christian art of Ravenna is charged with political implications in its inmost aesthetic structure and meaning. Here the religious dimension is only properly appreciated when implicit conceptions of social authority and hierarchy are kept in view. But early Christian eschatology like the art of Ravenna is charged with socio-political implications, though of a different kind, and reflects sociological factors which deserve attention.

Objections to a sociological approach to the phenomena of eschatology as to any aspect of Christian origins arise at the following points: (1) it suggests a kind of Marxist approach which particularly in our field has been tried and exploded; (2) it suggests a purely materialistic view of a topic which stands at the heart of the primitive revelation and may therefore be ruled out for dogmatic reasons; (3) it appeals to scientific categories and tests which like an ill-adapted sieve are not able to do justice to the material in question; and (4) we do not know enough about the ancient periods in question to explore this approach even if it be valid.

Yet we may call attention to one consideration which nevertheless encourages us in our task. When we meet with fervent eschatologically-minded groups and movements in the course of church history, especially in the recent period when documentation is possible, we often find an important correlation between them and critical economic and social situations. If some modern adventism has no such clear basis it can usually be put down to conscious or unconscious imitation of first-century attitudes and pieties.

The eschatological phenomena of post-Maccabean Judaism and early Christianity are no doubt very complex, and many factors are operative. But if we set aside derivative and devitalized examples and borrowed rhetorical and literary stage-properties, we may concentrate on the central matter of the consciousness of crisis and of καιρός, with its immediately related mythical mentality and mythology. This evolving experience with its evident creative power cries out for social-cultural explanation and it is either a regrettable incuriosity or worse which would here put sociological queries out of bounds, or would reserve the matter for purely theological explanation.

What misleads us here and what rightly prompts hesitation is the difficulty of applying modern sociological categories to an ancient period in which our distinctions of "economic," "social," "political," and "religious" were not made. It is entirely correct to question "economic determination" or "social explanation" of religious features in ancient or primitive cultures whose way of life knew no such differentiated aspects in the total pattern.

Our categories of social analysis do not adapt themselves easily to the Jewish theocratic situation or to the sacral political conceptions of the Hellenistic *polis* or the Roman Empire. Efforts a generation or two ago to describe the social factors in Jesus' setting and mission or to trace the "social origins" of the church are unpersuasive today because the historians in question modernized. To invoke such ideas as "proletariat" or "class struggle," to read in issues of "social justice" in terms of the twentieth century or even of the eighth-century prophets, to interpret the outlook of the Kingdom of God in terms of modern utopianism, to relate the common life of Acts 2 and 4-5 to modern communist ideas, or to see the otherworldly detachment of the Pauline churches in terms of the political and social abstention found in some modern pietism—all this was misleading. If we speak of the social determinations of early Christianity we must recognize that we have to do with social and political realities of an entirely unmodern character.

The mistake of the Marxist interpretation of early Christianity lay as much in the use of inappropriate modern yardsticks as in their crass materialism. But religious historians generally, not to mention theologians, also use questionable modern yardsticks in explaining the forces and movements in Judaism at the time of Christ : antinomies of liberal and conservative, applied for example to the Pharisees or to the Sadducees, or of nationalistic and cosmopolitan, applied to the Zealots on the one hand and again perhaps to the Sadducees on the other. There is truth in such categorization but the realities of ancient culture are thus disguised. For example, the Zealots were not activated by political emancipationism in our modern sense but by a "holy war" ideology and mystique which was at the same time political and religious. The so-called liberalism and humanism of the Pharisees have to be seen in a different light if we take account of the loss of meaning of their patterns for contemporary groups affected by new cultural conditions and ready to turn to the Essenes or to baptist sects or to the gospel of the Kingdom.

Therefore if we speak of social factors in connection with early Christian eschatology we can mean nothing so obvious and modern as economic conditions in the usual sense (poverty, triple taxation) or social conditions in the usual sense (overpopulation and slavery) or political conditions in the usual sense (the Herodian and Roman control and abuses). We must mean social or sociological factors in a first-century sense, where all such elements are part of a total cultural occasion which includes the religious heritage, and that whole situation is seen as at a point of radical crisis. Apocalyptic or highly dualistic eschatology as world-view and time-view arose out of such a general crisis in the inherited total way of life. The powerful mythology of imminent world-end and world-renewal arose out of a crisis in the tradition—loss of meaning, coherence, sense of reality— of which all that we mean by economic, social, political, cultural, religious phenomena were part. Günther Bornkamm speaks of a "world which had lost the present since . . . it lived between past and future, between tradition and promise or threat."[3] Similarly von Rad speaks of a situation at the time of the rise of the monarchy : ". . . a suspicious *Verwilderung* of [inherited symbols] . . . the word of the Lord was rare in those days . . . the 'edifice of meaning' had been radically transformed."[4]

In this light the question of documentation takes on a special character and the lack of statistics is not so great a bar to hypotheses as if we were dealing with social factors in a modern sense. We can be sure that such a world-shaping phenomenon as early Christian eschatology (with its Jewish antecedents and parallels) can be illuminated culturally and need not be surrendered to sheerly dogmatic explanations any more than modern utopias or millenarian movements. We should of course recognize that we have learned much from the standard investigations of the rise and development of eschatology and of the emergence of its apocalyptic-dualist forms. It is, however, too much to say that the common explanations tend to be rationalistic : disillusionment with the Davidic monarchy led to projection into the future of a Davidic restoration, or eschatological hope represented a projection upon the future of enthronement ideology, or the transcendental apocalyptic of Daniel and later writings is occasioned by new political constellations combined with a new cosmology. Such views do not go deep enough.

The problem has a parallel in that of the emergence and appeal of gnosticism. Hans Jonas is not satisfied to explain this great movement in terms solely of the genetic relationships of its mythology or of the history of ideas. In an important section of his work,[5] para-

---

[3] *Jesus von Nazareth* (Stuttgart, 1956), p. 52.
[4] *Theologie des Alten Testaments* (Munich, 1951), p. 47.
[5] *Gnosis und Spätaniker Geist* (Göttingen, 1934). Jonas laments the lack of concern (apart from that of Cumont) with the concrete social basis of the rise of

graph 17, "Zur Frage des Realgrundes (Psychologie-Soziologie)," he raises the question whether particular social and cultural circumstances in the Hellenistic period and early Empire can account for the enormous appeal of this similarly dualistic religious philosophy. His answer is that we do not know enough about the relation of concrete sociological patterns to the rise and diffusion of Gnosticism, especially in the East, to reach conclusions. But his discussion points convincingly to the fact that such factors were decisive if only we could trace them.

Eschatologies and adventisms, ancient and modern, differ greatly one from another and no single explanation will suit all of them. Yet when explanation is sought for their origin in the ancient period in question, it usually takes the form of dream-compensation for the victims of untoward earthly circumstances. Such a view can be presented with a disparaging intention or without. The Marxist intends disparagement. Many non-Marxist historians similarly assign escapist and compensatory motivations for the phenomenon, being conditioned in their historiography by the same rationalism that influences the Marxist. On the other hand, even such a social historian as Louis Finkelstein in his invaluable work on the Pharisees [6] has basically the same social explanation for the significant eschatological developments of the periods in question, without meaning to disparage the Hasidic and Pharisaic beliefs in resurrection, angels, world-renewal, etc. The following passage is representative :

> The fiercest of all the conflicts between Pharisee and Sadducee concerned the doctrine of the resurrection for in it the class conflict was most explicitly formulated. Crushed under the heel of the oppressor and exploiter, the artisan and trader of Jerusalem in the fourth century

---

Gnosticism. This neglect (and we may say the same for our own problem) is due in his view to the over-dominant philosophical and history-of-ideas perspective in the study of the history of religions. The social-genetic factor must be explored to understand Gnosticism, and it is not enough to speak of "a time of horror" in the related regions or of the "misery" of the common man. One must go deeper into the cultural causes of the existential attitude that transpires in Gnosticism. We are not well documented for this task in the East, Jonas continues, but in the West we know that there was a dying world ready for an a-cosmic salvation; a world in which there had been for the individual a "loss of role" and therefore of responsibility, and therefore of meaning and self-fulfillment. In the East, he suggests, one must postulate a "deep vital movement," a "new mythos in course of creation," a "particular social group structure" among Parthians and Jews or among groups of them.

[6] *The Pharisees: The Sociological Background of Their Faith*, Vols. 1 and 2 (Philadelphia, 1938.)

B.C.E. sought compensation in an ideal world beyond the grave, where all human inequalities would be leveled down before the overwhelming power of God. . . . An abstract immortality might satisfy the philosopher; the hungry slum dweller of Jerusalem could be comforted by nothing less than the Egyptian and Persian doctrine of physical resurrection and restitution.[7]

Dr. Finkelstein's notable venture into the sociology of our period is very refreshing and instructive. His conclusions, at least in the area of eschatology, however, are handicapped (it would seem) by a characteristic misunderstanding of eschatological mentality and rhetoric common to many historians of the liberal period, a misunderstanding which tends to see it in idealistic and quasi-aesthetic terms. This is a misunderstanding of "mythos." For example, in connection with the acceptance by the "plebeian" group of Jews in exile and later of the elaborate angelology and symbolism, etc., enhancing the glory of the court of Jahweh as not only "king of kings" but as "King of the kings of kings," Dr. Finkelstein speaks of "this magnificent imagery" which satiated "the Jewish cobbler sitting at his awl in Jerusalem, as in Babylon or Ecbatana," and which fortified him to endure with patience and contempt the derision heaped upon him by Persian and Greek. "He had a secret . . .," he knew of "phalanxes of immortal angels." The doctrine of angels met a "deep-seated psychological need."[8] At another point Dr. Finkelstein, with Isaiah 24-27 and late elements of Joel and Zachariah in mind, writes, "Thus wisdom and art combined to transform the prophet into the apocalyptist," and speaks of "sound pedagogy, effective rhetoric and personal prudence."[9] What we would specially note here is that the heightening transcendental expression of eschatology is seen as the outcome of a rhetorical option corresponding to an irreproachable demand for other-worldly compensations when the world's difficulties become too great.

No doubt these various judgments of the author have a certain validity with respect to particular periods or writings. But eschatological myth in its significant expressions is not just rhetoric and its central impulse is not that of rationalistic compensation. We have to do with a great variety of movements and prophecies or oracles, whether Jewish and Christian. We see the myths in all stages from the most spontaneous and ecstatic to the most reflective and derivative, from the most creative to the most slavishly wooden. We have to do especially with the very radical break between the old prophetic eschatology and the transcendental crisis eschatology associated with apocalyptic and with the new cosmology. The sociological factors involved will be highly various just as the literary sources are. But the more significant eschatological developments represented real gains in man's grasp of his history and destiny, corresponding to lived experience, and were not mere poetic consolation prizes and fictions.

It is of interest here that Frederick C. Grant, who has all along offered us the most thorough analysis of strictly social and economic factors in the environment of Palestine and who has characterized in an illuminating way the "agrarian ethic" of Jesus, nevertheless must finally deprecate the importance of such factors when he makes his final judgment as to the causes of the rise of the gospel, at least so far as concerns the imperial background. Here it is insisted that religious factors have the final word.

> It is less than ever possible, nowadays, to represent early Christianity as a revolutionary social (or social-economic) movement. Although, as we insist, religion is always conditioned by the world in which it lives, including the economic factor in that world, it is clear that Christianity was from the very beginning a purely religious movement, a cult, a body of beliefs and practices centered in something else than the economic welfare or well-being of any racial, national, or social group.[10]

Professor Grant identifies the spread of Christianity in the Empire especially with

> its message of hope for men living in this impermanent and not too secure world; with means of grace for those who realized their inability to master themselves or to rise above their surroundings; with an assurance of forgiveness for the penitent, and of release from the burden of sin and guilt; above all with a spirit of tenderness and compassion, 'the loving kindness of God our Savior' and his good will

[10] "The Economic Background of the New Testament," *The Background of the New Testament and its Eschatology*, ed. by W. D. Davies and D. Daube (Cambridge, 1956), p. 101. See also Grant, *An Introduction to New Testament Thought* (New York, 1950), pp. 27-28.

toward man combined with 'the meekness and gentleness of Christ.'[11]

Professor Grant well documents the fact that during the first century A.D. economic conditions were favorable and steadily improving in the Empire as a whole, with the exception of Palestine, and that socialistic sterotypes about a crushed Christian proletariat are entirely mistaken. Our view, however, is that the sociological, motivating occasions for the early Christian sense of crisis and fulfillment were not social in the sense of property, slavery, persecution, etc., but in a deeper and more comprehensive sense were appropriate to ancient life-patterns. Thus understood, "hope for men living in this impermanent and not too secure world" can be indistinguishably social-political and spiritual, and the same holds for "means of grace for those who realized their inability to master themselves or to rise above their surroundings."[12]

We have urged that the interrelations in our period of special social circumstances and of apocalyptic-eschatological conceptions should be viewed in the light of analogous social-religious phenomena in other cultures and periods. Crisis mentality dramatizing itself in various cosmic and psychological dualisms, in various spatial, temporal and moral images, is not confined to Palestine and the early Roman Empire. The whole complex of allied conceptions— rival angelic and demonic hosts, Satanism, demonic possession, mythologies of disorder in nature, ideologies of world end and world transformation—all such can be better understood in the light of social psychology, of course with full account taken of varying views of man and the world and of particular local factors. Thus the eschatological representations will differ as between, say, Isaiah 24-27, Qumran, the Book of Revelation, or the outlook of Florence at the time of Savonarola. Nevertheless all these throw light upon the main question.

We may well take into account modern parallels in European and American history : for example, Karl Mannheim's description of transcendental ideologies, and especially of chiliasm among the Anabaptists.[13] Similarly, the English Puritans and Levellers as

---

[11] Grant, "Economic Background," p. 114.

[12] Dr. Sherman E. Johnson discusses in an interesting way Professor Grant's characterization of Jesus' ministry as "the last great agrarian movement of antiquity" and enlarges the theme by venturing a sociological interpretation of the origins of Christianity, especially with reference to the dehumanization and and cheapness of life in the period. *Jesus in His Homeland* (New York, 1957); see especially pp. 106-109 and pp. 121-122.

[13] *Ideology and Utopia* (New York, 1930), pp. 215-216.

well as the founders of New England all in one way or another held views with regard to the fulfillment of history and its imminence which are of interest.[14] Even pathological group-hysterias are significant for our purpose. The history of the Church offers us examples of group neuroses or epidemics of fanaticism associated with the great plague or other calamities in which the public imagination is ready to identify Satan or the anti-Christ, to antici- pate the last Judgment, and to people the world with angels and demons and to resort to flagellations and witch hunts. In the United States during the great depression of the nineteen-thirties, social psychologists documented the inseparable relation of orgiastic apocalypticism with economic distress, or more widely with chang- ing social patterns.[15] While all this is familiar, we should be ready to recognize its bearing on biblical eschatology also.

We may even derive suggestions from observation of the neurotic psychology of the individual. It is well known that the clinic supplies us with not infrequent cases of individuals obsessed with the expectation of the end of the world, Messiah complexes, etc. We should not dismiss them as purely imitative and socially sug- gested. Dr. Anton T. Boisen has shown the correlation of such cases with problems of self-identification and vocation-finding of normal individuals in situations of social incoherence.[16] Such examples are not recalled to disparage the eschatological mentality but to illuminate it. Boisen, for example, makes clear that the crisis eschatologies of the clinic often have a highly constructive role and outcome. The structure of the eschatological mentality is not to be confused with its aberrations.

Late Jewish and early Christian eschatologies, as we find them in the major figures and documents, are conditioned by crisis situations (Daniel, Enoch, Qumran, the Baptist, Jesus, the primitive church), and it is not enough to identify these with either political persecution or economic pressures on the one hand or with "religious" factors on the other. The crises were religio-cultural whether in Palestine or in the Hellenistic pagan setting. The fantasy-like but yet often healthy projection of dramatic symbol suggesting the dissolution of the usual categories of time, space and causation reflect social- cultural incoherence, anomie and loss of meaning. As Ernst Fuchs

---

[14] Wilder, *Eschatology and Ethics in the Teaching of Jesus* (New York, 1950), pp. 24-25.

[15] Cf. W. R. Cross, *The Burned-Over District* (Ithaca, N.Y., 1950), chapters 17-18; also see Anton T. Boisen, *Religion in Crisis and Custom* (New York, 1945, 1955).

[16] Boisen, *op. cit.*

says in his *Hermeneutik*, "the place of myth is where the law of the *Grundlosen* rules," where "the forms of life are fluid."[17] I take this to mean that dynamic eschatological conceptions arise in this kind of situation. The eschatological mood represents a radical spiritual and cultural effort of a group (or an individual) to overcome disorder and to define meaning, and to give body to possibilities and to the future, as well as to come to terms with dynamic and radical changes in the conditions of existence. The background for this in the centuries before and after Christ was the loss of meaning and relationship of many groups, whether in Jewish or pagan life. So Mannheim can say that chiliasm arose in a "period of tremendous disintegration."[18] Such elements as poverty, slavery, class or social frustration, persecution, were only elements in the more general crisis. The hopes defined in the inevitably symbolic way were not escapist fantasies but were healthy and creative just as they were grounded in the social traditions of Jewish covenant theology, which, indeed, was later fused with Gentile civic and imperial ideals.

[17] (Bad Cannstatt, 1954), p. 169.
[18] *Op. cit.*, p. 226.

VIII | *S. Vernon McCasland*
UNIVERSITY OF VIRGINIA

"THE BLACK ONE"

As is well known, the name Satan, which was used only a few times in the Old Testament (II Chron. 21:1; Job 1:4—2:7; Zech. 3:1), is a standard name in the New Testament.[1] Originally it meant simply *the adversary*, but finally it became the most common name for the arch-spirit of evil. We are not concerned with Beliar (II Cor. 6:15) or with Beelzebul, which appears in Mark 3:22 and its parallels (Matt. 10:25; 12:24, 27; Luke 11:15, 18, 19), as alternate names of Satan. As they stand they are metonyms, but each of them at first probably was the name of some particular spirit or deity. Another picturesque and familiar metonym is Destroyer, which occurs in Rev. 9:11 as Abaddon, from Hebrew, or Apollyon, from Greek.

The Devil as a metonym or alternate name was first used in biblical literature in Wisdom of Solomon 2:24, but after that it frequently appeared in late apocryphal documents.[2] In the New Testament the name Devil is used so often as to be in no need of documentation.

Certain metonyms indicate that Satan is prince over a realm. In Mark 3:22 and its parallels in Matthew and Luke he is the Prince of demons. John 12:31 refers to him as the Prince of this world, but in Eph. 2:2 he is Prince of the powers of the air. I Tim. 5:14 makes him simply the Adversary (τῷ ἀντικειμένῳ), which shows that the author recalled the original meaning of the word Satan, and I Pet. 5:8 indicates the same thing.

It was also Wisdom of Solomon 2:24 which first identified the

---

[1] A research of mine published about a decade ago dealt with" Some New Testament Metonyms for God" (*JBL*, LXVIII [1949], 99-113), and the present paper is an extension of that study to include New Testament metonyms for Satan.

[2] The Books of Adam and Eve 10:2, 12:1, 13:1; 17:1. 3; Apoc. Mos. 15:3 16:1, 2, 5; 17:4; 21:3; II En. 31:3; III Bar. 4:8.

serpent in Eden with Satan. Thus this writer states, "But through the Devil's envy death came into the world, and those who belong to his party experience it."[3] II Baruch 4:3-6 reveals a pair of dragons, one of which is Satan and the other Hades. The identification of the serpent with Satan is reflected in Paul's observation in II Cor. 11:3, "As the serpent beguiled Eve in his craftiness," and also in Rom. 16:20, "The God of peace shall bruise Satan under your feet shortly." But the idea appears most clearly in Rev. 12:9, "And he cast out the great dragon, the ancient serpent, the one who is called the Devil and Satan, the deceiver of the whole world"; and we are informed in Rev. 20:3 that the dragon was bound for a thousand years.

Another frequent and well recognized metonym for Satan is the Evil One.[4]

All of the metonyms for Satan listed above have been recognized and catalogued, but I propose some now which, to my knowledge, have not been so recognized before. The first of these is the word Sin as it is used in the seventh chapter of Romans. This is the passage in which Paul works out his penetrating analysis of human personality into three struggling elements, Law, Ego and Sin, an insight which was reproduced by Sigmund Freud in his concepts of the Superego, Ego and Id. Paul's meaning becomes very clear as soon as one recognizes that Sin, as the word is used here, is a metonym for Satan. Sin is a malignant living being which resides in the flesh and wages a constant, desperate and usually successful battle to prevent the Ego from keeping the Law. For example, Paul says, "sin beguiled . . . and slew me," "sold under sin," "sin which dwelleth in me," "with the mind indeed, serve the law of God; but with the flesh the law of sin." The last words in particular show beyond doubt that in Paul's mind Sin is balanced against God. It must therefore be a metonym for Satan.

Paul used this same manner of speech again in Gal. 3:22, where he writes, "But the scripture shut up all things under sin, that the promise in Jesus Christ might be given to them that believe." The Revised Standard Version says "consigned all things to sin." It is evident that here Paul treats Sin as a personal monster; and a somewhat similar image lurks in the words of I Cor. 15:56, "The sting of death is sin; and the power of sin is the law."

The use of Sin as a metonym for Satan is not limited to Paul. We see it in the lines of Wisdom of Solomon 10:3, "When an upright man was sold, she did not abandon him, but delivered him from

---

[3] E. J. Goodspeed, *The Apocrypha, An American Translation* (Chicago, 1938).
[4] Cf. Matt. 6:13; 13:19; 13:38; John 17:15; etc.

sin." Moreover, the same idiom is used in *Pirke Aboth* 2:1, "And keep in view three things, and thou wilt not come into the clutches of sin; know what is above thee, an eye that sees and an ear that hears, and all thy deeds written in a book."[5] The concept appears also in 3:1.

Another unrecognized metonym for Satan is Darkness. Light has been associated with goodness and darkness with evil the world over, and this is certainly true of biblical literature. The words of Isaiah 9:2 are typical:

> The people that walked in darkness have seen a great light: They that dwelt in the land of the shadow of death, upon them hath the light shined.

The fact that criminals ply their wicked trade at night was well known; it was generally believed that evil spirits prowled in darkness, and it was customary to associate blackness and gloom with Sheol. It was only natural, therefore, that Satan should be delineated against this dark background, and it appears to have been inevitable that in time the darkness with which he was habitually associated should become his metonym. One would not expect to find this metonym in the Old Testament, for the belief in Satan barely made its appearance there. Yet this association did occur in other late Jewish literature. It is clearly present in some of the recently discovered literature of the Dead Sea Scrolls.[6] In "The War between the Sons of Light and the Sons of Darkness" the idea is obvious, but it is clear also in the symbol of the *two ways*, which is basic in the *Manual of Discipline*.[7] In such a context Light and Darkness are metonyms for God and Satan.

While at present we do not know the origin of these new things in the Dead Sea Scrolls, they throw light on similar ideas in the New Testament and other early Christian writings. To say the least, a two-ways document reflected in the *Manual of Discipline* belongs to the same family as similar Christian documents referred to below.

In the New Testament itself, Jesus says in Luke 22:53, "but this is your hour, and the power of darkness." Acts 26:18 reports that Paul said "that they may turn from darkness to light and from the power of Satan unto God." We find Paul saying in Cor. 1:13, "who delivered us out of the power of darkness," and in Eph. 5:11, "have no fellowship with the unfruitful works of darkness." All of these passages are immediately illuminated when we recognize that

---

[5] R. H. Charles, *Apocrypha and Pseudepigrapha of the Old Testament* (Oxford, 1913), II, 694 f.

[6] Millar Burrows, *The Dead Sea Scrolls* (New York, 1955).

[7] S. V. McCasland, "The Way," *JBL*, LXXII (1958), 222-230.

Darkness is a metonym for Satan.

It remained for the author of Barnabas to bring this treatment of Satan to its artistic culmination. First he takes the idea of the two Ways in xviii. 1-2 as follows:

> Now let us pass on to another lesson and teaching. There are two Ways of teaching and power, one of Light and one of Darkness. And there is a great difference between the two Ways. For over the one are set light-bringing angels of God, but over the other angels of Satan. And the one is the Lord from eternity to eternity, and the other is the ruler of the present time of iniquity. [8]

The ideas appear also in the *De Doctrina Apostolorum* i. 1, thus: *Vitae duae sunt in saeculo vitae et mortis, lucis et tenebrarum.* Moreover, they are found in modified form in both the Didache and the *Life of Schnudi* i. 1. [9]

In Barnabas iv. 9 and xx.1, however, the metonymic treatment of the arch-spirit of evil becomes complete—at least it achieves esthetic fullness—when Satan is referred to as the Black One. In iv. 9 we have, "Wherefore let us pay heed in the last days, for the whole time of our life and faith will profit us nothing, unless we resist, as becomes the sons of God in this present evil time, against the offences which are to come, that the Black One may have no opportunity of entry." The author, in xx. 1, reintroduces the notion of the two Ways thus: "But the Way of the Black One is crooked and full of cursing, for it is the way of death eternal with punishment, and in it are the things that destroy their soul." [10]

This is a perfect example of the origin and development of one particular metonym, as well as of the nature of metonyms in general. First was the terrifying nature of darkness. Then there was the well known fact that lawless persons prefer to operate at night; and the primitive philosophy of animism peopled the darkness with evil spirits. When Satan finally came into biblical thinking it was only natural to assign night especially to him and his hosts. It was a logical step then for darkness, which was so often associated with Satan, to become his metonym. Once this step was taken, it was almost inevitable that some imaginative person would designate Satan as the Black One. That distinction appears to belong to the author of the Greek Barnabas, who said quite simply ὁ μέλας.

[8] Kirsopp Lake, *The Apostolic Fathers* (New York, 1912), I, 401.

[9] The four documents, Barnabas, Doctrina, Didache and Schnudi, are presented in parallel columns by E. J. Goodspeed in *The Apostolic Fathers* (New York, 1950), pp. 206-310.

[10] Kirsopp Lake, *op. cit.*, I, 353 and 407.

IX | *Sherman E. Johnson*
CHURCH DIVINITY SCHOOL
OF THE PACIFIC

CHRISTIANITY
IN SARDIS

I

Christianity in Sardis is first known from the letters to the seven churches in the Book of Revelation. When the apocalyptic prophet John writes (Rev. 3:1-7), the church in the ancient Lydian city may have existed for some time, for it has the name of being alive but is dead. John recognizes that in Sardis there are still a few who have not soiled their garments and are worthy, but the church must awake and strengthen what little remains. Its decadence may have been a relapse into paganism or into the error of the Nicolaitans mentioned in the letters to Pergamum and Thyatira (Rev. 2:15, 20 ff.), which involved the eating of foods sacrificed to pagan gods. If this was the situation, Paul's teaching about Christian freedom may have led to what John considered a dangerous laxity. But we cannot prove any connection between Paul and the earliest church in Sardis. Of the seven churches of the Apocalypse, only two— Ephesus and Laodicea—are known to have had any connection with the great apostle. It is possible, of course, that on the so-called third missionary journey Paul went through the Hermus valley on his way to Ephesus; but, as I have argued elsewhere,[1] the most logical route for him to take was past Laodicea and down along the Maeander river. A third possibility is that he came through the Caÿster valley, but this would have involved another mountain pass, and the towns along this route were not as important as those in the other two valleys.

On the other hand, John represents a highly Jewish type of Christianity, and the churches to which he writes are closely

---

[1] S. E. Johnson, "Laodicea and Its Neighbors," *BA*, XIII (1950), 1-18.

related to Judaism. Inscriptions from Sardis show, as we might expect, that there was a Jewish community there, but such monuments are very few. It is interesting, therefore, that in 1958 an inscription referring to the god Sabazios was found in the northwest part of the village of Sart-Mustafa by a member of the American expedition, John Washeba, conservator of antiquities of the Fogg Art Museum, and Halil Akyar, his local assistant. This fragmentary stele, which will be published fully at a later time, was apparently dedicated by Menophilos, son of Menophilos, and gives the name of the god in the form Sauazios.[2] A king Eumenes is also mentioned, and the name Zeus in the dative case appears toward the end.

The Eumenes of this inscription is quite possibly Eumenes II (197-159 B.C.), whose consort Stratonice brought the worship of Sabazios from her homeland, Cappadocia.[3] The style of writing of the newly found stele is very similar to a previously published inscription which Buckler and Robinson dated to the time of Eumenes II.[4] Δıí suggests that at Sardis, as at Pergamum, Sabazios is identified with Zeus. This is not surprising, since elsewhere in Lydia Zeus-Sabazios inscriptions appear.[5]

Sabazios is an elusive god with many connections. He is sometimes associated with Men and with the Great Mother of Asia Minor, also with Demeter and Persephone.[6] He is also identified with Dionysos, and both in the forms Zeus-Sabazios and Dionysos-Sabazios he is further equated with the God of the Jews. This is so well known and has been discussed so frequently[7] that I shall mention only the Sabazios cult of Apameia (Celaenae, the modern Dinar), located in Phrygia east of Colossae and Laodicea. Noah and the ark appear on coins of the city, and according to local legend the mountain on which the ark rested after the flood was behind Apameia. Noah was noted for having planted the first vines and for getting drunk from their produce, and, according to Plut-

---

[2] Sauazios or Saoazos is an Anatolian form of the name; see, e.g., M. P. Nilsson, *Geschichte der griechischen Religion*, II (Munich, 1950), 631, 633; but the form Sabazios is also found in inscriptions from Lydia; see L. Robert, *Hellenica*, VI (Limoges, 1948), 111-13; VII (1949), 45 f. The name Menophilos is frequently found in Sardis inscriptions.

[3] M. Fränkel, *Die Inschriften von Pergamon* (Berlin, 1890), No. 248. This inscription shows the attachment of the Attalids to the Sabazios cult.

[4] W. H. Buckler and D. M. Robinson, *Sardis*, VII, 1 (Leiden, 1932), No. 88.

[5] See, e.g., Karl Buresch, *Aus Lydien* (Leipzig, 1898), p. 74.

[6] Nilsson, *op. cit.*, pp. 631-34; Buresch, *op. cit.*, p. 62 f.

[7] See, e.g., Nilsson, *op. cit.*, p. 636; F. Cumont, "Les mystères de Sabazios et le judaïsme," *Comptes-rendus, académie des inscriptions* (Paris, 1906), 63-79; W. O. E. Oesterley in S. H. Hooke, ed., *The Labyrinth* (London, 1935).

arch, Dionysos-Sabazios, the patron of viticulture, was assimilated to Yahweh. Certainly there was an important Jewish community in the city which had been absorbed by the local culture.

While some of the Jews of Sardis seem to have maintained their identity, it is possible that others worshipped Zeus-Sabazios just as those at Apameia had followed the god in his form of Dionysos. The Jews of Phrygia had a reputation for loyalty to the Seleucid dynasty, which had settled them in so prosperous a land, and it is possible that in Lydia this tradition of loyalty to the monarchy was transferred to the Attalids. This would tend to encourage the worship of Sabazios. Such a background would make a relapse into paganism on the part of Jewish Christians much easier to understand.

The author of the Book of Revelation was intimately acquainted with western Asia Minor. One of his most curious characteristics is that he is a very Jewish kind of Christian who regards Christians as the true Jews, thoroughly familiar with the Old Testament and the apocalyptic tradition, and apparently an observer of the so-called apostolic decree of Acts 15:23-29 which forbade the eating of food offered to pagan gods, while on the other hand he is bitterly opposed to orthodox Judaism and calls it a "synagogue of Satan" (Rev. 2:9; 3:9). Asia Minor Christianity continued to take this ambivalent attitude, so much so that Ignatius of Antioch protested against Judaizing in any form, and as late as the fourth century the Council of Laodicea found it desirable to adopt a canon condemning those who Judaized by abstaining from work on Saturday.[8]

II

Ignatius says nothing of a church in Sardis, but he writes to churches at Philadelphia and Smyrna and in the Maeander valley to the south (Magnesia and Tralles) as well as at Ephesus. Did Sardis have no bishop at this time, or was its bishop unfriendly to Ignatius and his associates? The bishop of Antioch makes a clear distinction between Judaism and Christianity (he is the first known writer to use the latter word, e.g., *Magn.* 10:1, 3), and when we first learn of a bishop in Sardis, a little before A.D. 170, we find that he too sees the Church as definitely opposed to the synagogue, for he fastens the entire blame for the crucifixion of Christ on the Jewish people when he writes his *Homily on the Passover.*

Melito is one of the most important of early Christian writers. Except for the *Homily*, later to be discussed, we have only fragments

[8] Johnson, *op. cit.*, p. 18; cf. also Johnson in P. M. Suzuki (ed.), *Theologia Oecumenica in Honor of William Enkichi Kan* (Tokyo, 1958), pp. 35-44.

of a few of his books.[9] He was an important commentator on the Old Testament, which he uses in a typological fashion somewhat reminiscent of the Epistle of Barnabas. His *Book of Extracts*, mentioned by Eusebius, includes a list of the authorized Scriptures of the Old Covenant, which is an important document for the Christian history of the Old Testament canon.

Melito's style contains Semitic elements, as would be natural for a man given to reading the Old Testament. But there are other interesting traits in it. He uses analogies from nature and human society; for example, hot metals are baptized with water, the earth is baptized by rain, the sun plunges into the ocean. He loves contrasts and paradoxes: the judge is judged, the invisible one is seen, the immeasurable one is held in a measure, the impassible suffers (*On Soul and Body*). These paradoxes are very like Ignatius (e.g., *Eph.* 7:2). Both men are influenced in their writing by the florid Asian style which arose in the Maeander valley before the Christian Era and at this time was gradually being superseded among pagan literati by the sober Atticistic fashion.

The *Homily on the Passover* is a most remarkable tractate.[10] Eusebius dates its writing as follows: "When Servillius Paulus was proconsul of Asia, at the season when Sagaris suffered martyrdom, there arose a great discussion in Laodicea concerning the *Pascha*, which fell in due season in those days" (*H. E.* iv. 26). We have already spoken of the Judaizing tendencies of the Maeander valley. The Quartodeciman movement is connected with them, and Melito is one of the most prominent defenders of this liturgical peculiarity. His Christian Passover was celebrated on the 14th of Nisan, the Jewish date, and both the Cross and Resurrection are commemorated in this paschal sermon, though the emphasis is on Christ as risen. When Polycrates of Ephesus had his famous controversy with Victor, about A.D. 180, Melito was already dead, for Polycrates speaks of "Melito the eunuch who in all things lived in

---

[9] Besides the fragments in Eusebius, several are published in E. J. Goodspeed, *Die ältesten Apologeten* (Göttingen, 1914). Several important pieces are translated by R. M. Grant, *Second-Century Christianity* (London, 1946).

[10] The *editio princeps* is by Campbell Bonner, *The Homily on the Passion of Melito Bishop of Sardis* (London, 1940); but cf. the new edition by Bernhard Lohse, *Die Passa-Homilie des Bischofs Meliton von Sardes*, *Textus Minores*, XXIV (Leiden, 1958), with good bibliography. An additional manuscript, from the Bodmer collection, has now been published; cf. M. Testuz, ed., *Papyrus Bodmer XIII. Méliton de Sardes, Homelie sur la Pâque* (Cologny-Genève, 1960).

the Holy Spirit, who lies at Sardis, awaiting the visitation from heaven, when he shall rise from the dead" (*H. E.* v. 24. 5).[11]

The *Homily* makes clear what Polycrates must have meant by Melito living "in the Holy Spirit," for in the remarkable peroration of this sermon he is not only a bishop and a teacher but a prophet. Here he steps out of his own character and speaks words of the risen Christ, just as John did in his letters to the seven churches, and as Ignatius must have done in Philadelphia, as he says, "When I was among you, I spoke with a great voice, with the voice of God" (*Philad.* 7:1). Christian prophets were known in Phrygia and Lydia, particularly in Philadelphia, and by Melito's time the prophetic movement had erupted into Montanism. Indeed in these parts of Asia Minor there were both men and women prophets, some of whom were claimed as their own by both orthodox and Montanists. Such a figure as Melito, ascetic, passionate and learned, with his eloquence and vivid rhetoric, must have made a profound impression on the churches of Asia Minor by his other writings as well.

In Asia Minor there had been persecution of Christians from time to time, the martyrdom of Polycarp being an outstanding example which illustrates, by the way, the hostility between church and synagogue in spite of, perhaps because of, the Judaizing tendencies which continued. Eusebius quotes the letter of Antoninus Pius to the *koinon* of Asia bidding people to stop the persecutions (*H. E.* iv. 13) : "That such was the course of events is a fact further testified by Melito, bishop of the church at Sardis, who was well known at that time : as is clear from what he has said in the Apology for our faith which he addressed to the emperor Verus."

This notice of Eusebius gives particular interest to a dedicatory inscription excavated at Sardis during the 1958 campaign. Here it should be explained that only a small portion of the ancient city has as yet been uncovered. The ruins of Sardis extend from just west of the Pactolus to a point about two miles to the east where two parallel walls, built of massive masonry, stand above the surface. On the north the line of a city wall can be traced among the orchards of the Hermus plain. On the southeast the ruins are bounded by the Acropolis, where some ruined walls still stand, and there are indications of settlement west of it for a mile or two. It appears that the city occupied at least two square miles, exclusive of the cemetery on the Necropolis hill, the tombs of the Lydian kings (Bin Tepe)

---

[11] Grant, *op. cit.*, p. 69, suggests, no doubt rightly, that "eunuch" means only that Melito was a celibate.

north of the Hermus river, and whatever villages may have lain outside the city. The Princeton expedition of 1910-14 excavated the temple of Artemis and its immediate environs and also dug a number of Lydian tombs; otherwise its efforts were mainly confined to surface exploration and the recording of monuments above ground.

The expedition of 1958 dug a test trench south of the Artemis temple and made another sounding on a hill to the temple's north, but its most important achievement was that it began the systematic investigation of other parts of the city. The walls of the structure at the end of the city (the so-called CG) were partly cleared, and the archaeologists also partially excavated Building B, a complicated late Roman structure, evidently a gymnasium, which lies just north of the main automobile road, some Byzantine shops adjoining it to the south, and also a small area south of the road. In the last-named place excavation seems to have touched for the first time the part of the city principally inhabited from the Lydian period through the Byzantine. It is probable that the ancient road through Sardis was located not far from the present highway, in other words where the ground begins to rise toward Mount Tmolus to the south, where the road would be high enough to be fairly dry through the winter.[12]

The 1959 excavations established the presence of Lydian buildings in a cliff along the Pactolus river north of the Artemis temple. Work was continued in Building B, in the House of Bronzes, and in the CG area, where it was found that a Roman bath had at one time been built into the two large masonry structures. In addition, new areas were excavated on both sides of Building B and on an upper terrace southeast of the House of Bronzes and near the city wall.[13] Still other parts of the ancient city, including Lydian areas, were investigated in the 1960 campaign, but at the time of this writing information had not yet been released for publication.

The dedicatory inscription found in 1958 is a marble base which apparently served as a pedestal for a statue of the emperor Lucius Verus (161-169), the co-emperor of Marcus Aurelius.[14] It stands in the center of a semicircular platform in the southern apse of the south hall of Building B, only a few yards from the

---

[12] Cf. G. M. A. Hanfmann, *BASOR*, 154 (April, 1959), 5-35; Hanfmann and A. H. Detweiler, *Archaeology*, XII (1959), 53-61.

[13] Cf. Hanfmann, *BASOR*, 157 (Feb., 1960), 8-43.

[14] Photograph, description and translation are given by S. E. Johnson, "Preliminary Epigraphic Report on the Inscriptions Found at Sardis in 1958," *BASOR*, 158 (April, 1960), 6-11.

modern highway. The inscription begins by saying that Sardis, which was twice νεωκόρος (temple-warden), had honored Verus, and goes on to state that Claudius Antonius Lepidus, high priest of Asia and first treasurer, had by virtue of his office taken charge of arrangements for the gymnasium. There are various problems of translation and historical interpretation which need not concern us here: it is sufficient to point out that the inscription confirms the conjecture of Buckler and Robinson that Sardis had already received a second neocorate in the reign of Antoninus Pius.[15] The wardenship probably refers to a temple for imperial worship, and it has long been known that Sardis, like other cities of proconsular Asia, was devoted to this cult.

Lucius Verus had left Rome in 162 because Vologases III of Parthia had attacked Armenia. He was successful in a campaign against this monarch and in the spring of 166 he set out on his return to Rome. We know that on the way he stopped at Ephesus, where a monument was set up to celebrate his victory and he was given an official reception. It is therefore possible that he visited Sardis and that the statue and inscription were erected some time in 166 or 167.

The imperial cult constituted a threat and problem of conscience of the utmost seriousness to the Christians of Asia Minor. The combination of Sardis' second neocorate, the toleration granted by Antoninus Pius, the desire to show proper loyalty to the Empire while defending Christians against forced conformity to emperor worship, and finally the visit of Verus to Asia Minor, provides a perfect occasion for Melito to compose his *Apology*. It is not impossible that the Sardis bishop personally presented the emperor with a copy of his book. The coincidence in time suggests that dedications of such books to persons in high office were not mere literary conventions. Melito and other Christians hoped that the emperors would consider their arguments seriously and favorably.

III

The years when the church in Sardis flourished most outwardly and materially were from 325 to 1402, when Tamerlane destroyed the city. After that time Sardis shrank to a village, as it is today. As late as the seventeenth century there were still Christians there, but they had neither a church nor a priest; at present the only religion professed is Islam. Numerous episodes of the city's Christian history in the Byzantine period, together with lists of bishops and

---

[15] *Sardis*, VII, 1, Nos. 64, 72.

some source material, were collected by Germanos, metropolitan of Sardis and Pisidia, in a little volume published some years ago.[16] It is necessary to comment on only a few points and to supplement the written sources by allusion to some archaeological finds.

No Christian monuments from the third century have yet been discovered, unless Buckler and Robinson were right in identifying as a "crypto-Christian imprecation" of A.D. 215-280 the fragment of a stone which reads "he shall be accountable to God."[17]

By the beginning of the fourth century the bishop of Sardis was recognized as metropolitan of Lydia, and Artemidorus of Sardis was present at the Council of Nicaea.[18] Obviously an important cathedral church must have been built shortly after the end of the persecution, and a fragmentary inscription which may be as early as the fourth century was found in the debris of a late burial ground on the south side of the temple area. This reads προταναγνώστου, "[place] of the chief lector." No remains have been discovered of the church where it might have been placed.[19] There is, however, a small brick church with two apses built against the southeast corner of the great temple. When discovered it contained an altar in the shape of a plain stone table, and Butler regarded it as one of the earliest Christian churches in existence.[20] It was not much more than a chapel for neighborhood use.

There is hope of finding further archaeological evidence concerning the Sardis churches. Late in the 1958 campaign a small area was excavated south of the main highway and directly facing Building B. Here in the House of Bronzes, among other bronze objects, a shovel for embers surmounted by a cross was discovered.[21] Further clearing of Byzantine shops south of Building B in 1959 disclosed, in Shop SW 8, a marble tank or basin with two crosses with rounded bases cut on two frontal slabs. Resting south of the basin was a marble block that resembles a baptismal font. Hanfmann conjectured that the shop in its latest phase may have been

---

[16] Germanos, Ἱστορικὴ μελέτη περὶ τῆς ἐκκλησίας τῶν Σάρδεων (Constantinople, 1928), cf. V. Schultze, Altchristliche Städte und Landschaften, II, 2 (Gütersloh, 1926), pp. 145-56.

[17] Sardis, VII, 1, No. 164. It is of course possible that ὁ Θεός means only "the god in question."

[18] J. D. Mansi, Sacrorum conciliorum nova et amplissima collectio (Florence, 1759-81), II, 695; Severin Binius, Concilia generalia et provincialia, graeca et latina quotquot reperiri potuerunt (2nd ed., Cologne, 1618), I, 1, 282.

[19] Sardis, VII, 1, No. 188.

[20] Sardis, I, 1, pp. 112 ff.

[21] Hanfmann and Detweiler, op. cit., p. 59.

used as a chapel or baptistery.[22] It may be that further exploration of the area will disclose houses inhabited by ecclesiastical persons and possibly churches.

One naturally asks how early Sardis conformed to conciliar orthodoxy in doctrine and practice. After the Arian council of Ariminum and the semi-Arian council of Seleucia in 359, about fifty bishops who were partisans of the homoean Acacius met in Constantinople (360). They pronounced sentences of deposition on several bishops from whom they differed in doctrine; not, however, on the ground of doctrine but of violation of church order. Heortasius of Sardis was deposed because he had been ordained without the sanction of the other bishops of Lydia.[23] Heortasius, if not Nicene (as he may well have been), would thus seem to have been more orthodox by Nicene standards than those who sought to unseat him. That he was consecrated without the sanction of other Lydian bishops may mean that he and they did not agree in doctrine.

At the first session of the Council of Ephesus no bishop of Sardis is listed, but in the second session (Action 6), there is a subscription of "Meonius episcopus ecclesiae quae est Sardis Lydiae."[24] The historian Socrates says of Nestorius, who was condemned at this council, "With what calamities he visited the Quartodecimans throughout Asia, Lydia and Caria, and what multitudes perished in a popular tumult of which he was the cause at Miletus and Sardis, I think proper to pass by in silence."[25] Thus, although the first Nicene council had condemned the Quartodeciman custom, it still had its followers in Lydia more than a century later.

One Sardis inscription from the fifth or sixth century utters the prayer "May God protect the bishop," while another of the same period records a votive offering of two deacons named Zoetos and Iulianos.[26] A sixth-century inscription recorded the names, now lost, of pagans interned by order of the imperial judge Hyperechios. This is regarded as referring to a persecution which began in Lydia between 531 and 534.[27]

From this time on the ecclesiastical history of Sardis merges in that of the Byzantine Empire generally, and, as the city dwindled, its see decreased in prestige and influence. The most striking incident of later times occurred early in the ninth century and

---

[22] Hanfmann, *BASOR*, 157, pp. 32 f.

[23] Sozomen, *HE*, iv. 24.

[24] Mansi, *op. cit.*, IV, 1364; Binius, *op. cit.*, I, 2, 264.

[25] Socrates, *HE*, vii. 29.

[26] *Sardis*, VII, 1, Nos. 190, 189.

[27] *Ibid.*, No. 19.

centers in the bishop Euthymius, whom the Eastern Church regards as a saint and confessor. A powerful *strategos* cast his eye on an orphan girl who seems to have taken religious vows and tried to force her into marriage. Because Euthymius protected her he was deprived of his see and forced into a long exile. He was a zealous defender of the veneration of icons and suffered on this account also.[28] Thus at this point the see of Sardis comes into conflict with the state. The city's history reflects the varying currents of Christian history in Asia Minor.

[28] J. Pargoire, *L'église byzantine de 527 à 847* (2nd ed., Paris, 1905), pp. 268 f., 364.

X | *Mervin M. Deems*
BANGOR THEOLOGICAL
SEMINARY

EARLY CHRISTIAN
ASCETICISM

After the conquests of Alexander the Great the winds of religious
and cultural syncretism blew across the peoples of those Near
Eastern lands lying in the path of caravan or caravel. Palestine was
the center of this crossroads traffic. The attempted hellenization of
the Jews by Antiochus IV (Epiphanes), repulsed by an aroused
nation under the Maccabeans, had in a subtler manner begun to
penetrate through Sadducean leadership. Jews of the Diaspora
(and Antiochus had forwarded the planting of Jewish colonies)
became acquainted with the ways of the Gentiles by having to live
in their midst. Yet the Jew at home and abroad protected fiercely
his racial and religious characteristics. From the second century
B. C. Jewish literature reflected the hope and expectation of the
Day of Judgment and of the Lord when God, taking affairs into his
own hands, would overthrow the oppressor and begin a new age.
But for this objective the Jews in Palestine were neither united in
purpose nor agreed in plan.

I

The Jews were not ascetic. God created the world and it was good
and to be enjoyed. Man was to be fruitful and multiply. The body
was not evil, nor was there contrast, as in Greek thought, between
body and soul.[1] Early practices of continence and fasting may
reflect taboo. Later Judaism associated fasting and continence with
the prayer season, and for the maintenance of chastity a light diet
and abstinence from strong drink are advised.[2] Tobit proclaims
almsgiving a purge for sin (12:8). Sirach advocates the golden

---

[1] John A. T. Robinson, *The Body* (Chicago, 1952), p. 14.
[2] Test. XII Patr.: Reub. 1:10; Sim. 3:4; Jud. 15:4; Zeb. 4:2; Jos. 3:4 f.

mean, but the Wisdom of Solomon emphasizes the good life even though one's reward will be in the future. We even find the Platonic idea from Orphism that "a corruptible body weigheth down the soul, and the earthly frame lieth heavy on the mind that is full of cares" (9:15). The Testaments of the Twelve Patriarchs stresses the period of affliction preceding the intervention of God. Meantime, demons control this world and incite man to follow his evil inclination (*yeṣer*), which is to sin. Only devoted study of Torah can prevent this. [3]

As political, economic and social tensions increased along with disunity within the nation, the Jew looked forward to the end of the age and the intervention of God. Could this be prepared for and even accelerated by unusual attention to Torah? Could God's will be hastened, his Kingdom be *made* to come by decisive, revolutionary action? The Essenes attempted to answer affirmatively the first question, the Zealots the second.

Philo and Josephus inform us of some four thousand Essenes living in their own communities throughout Palestine and Pliny tells of a large settlement in the desert of Engedi. [4] Elsewhere I have delineated the ascetic life of Essenes and Therapeutae. [5] Suffice it to say that they renounced marriage (though Josephus knew of one group which married) and oaths, bathed often, wore white garments and lived apart from the world. According to Philo, the Therapeutae lived a contemplative life, each going to his own μοναστήριον to pray. Rigid fasting was insisted upon. The origin of these groups was obscure, as was that of the fiercely patriotic, revolutionary Zealots who, regardless of when they were founded, exhibited the same fervor as the Maccabees. Under the Romans no less than under the Seleucids, Jews would go to their death rather than give up Torah. Certainly Farmer is correct in saying that "among the Pharisees, Essenes, and Zealots there was substantial agreement on many if not most major points of doctrine" and "these three groups constituted the mainstream of the national resistance movement." [6]

The discovery of the Dead Sea Scrolls threw additional light

---

[3] *Qiddusin* 30b on Gen. 4:7. Cf. Ecclus. 21:11a.

[4] Philo, *Quod Omnis Probus Liber*, 12, 13; Josephus *Jewish War* I. iii. 5; II, viii. 2-13; *Ant.* XIII. x. 1, 2; XV. x. 5; XVIII. i. 5, etc.; Pliny *Nat. Hist.* v. 17.

[5] See my chapter on "The Sources of Christian Asceticism" in *Environmental Factors in Christian History* (Chicago, 1939). Here also may be found a brief and selected bibliography on the subject to that year.

[6] Cf. William Reuben Farmer, *Maccabees, Zealots, and Josephus* (New York, 1956), p. 190.

upon the environment of early Christianity. Most scholars believe the settlement at Qumran to have been Essene although there are dissimilarities as well as similarities. Our purpose is to note characteristics which "furnish a picture of the religious and cultural climate in which John the Baptist conducted his mission and in which Jesus was initially reared."[7] Those who entered the movement undertook a covenant with God, knowing that in the final war between Light and Darkness the faithful would be victorious after forty years of messianic disturbance. The Sons of Light, now in exile, will return, and since the holy angels march with them, they must be "unimpaired in spirit and flesh and ready for the day of vengeance." Actually, the warfare is incessant, with the Brotherhood striving manfully to conquer evil. Striking indeed are the references in the *Manual of Discipline* to the two spirits (good and evil), or inclinations, appointed to man by God. Created by him these spirits form the foundation of every act, instigate every deed and direct every thought.[8] Those who are of the enlightenment pursue the healthful and rewarding "way" (it is described as a "way") of truth. But to the spirit of perversity belongs the way of destruction. "It is in these ways that men needs must walk" and between the two is "eternal enmity."[9] The Brotherhood was governed by a group of presbyters, described as three priests and twelve laymen "schooled to perfection," but the entire community being "a fabric of holiness" by righteous living could effect atonement for the whole earth so that God could "shrive the earth of its guilt."[10] The Covenanters carried on a deeply religious communal life for the sake of righteousness and looked forward to the time when God would raise up the Teacher of Righteousness and when evil would be finally defeated.

It would hardly have been possible for one living in Palestine in the first century of our era to have missed the surge of piety and

[7] Theodore H. Gaster, *The Dead Sea Scriptures* (New York, 1956), p. 12. I use here Gaster's translation of the Scrolls. Cf. also Oscar Cullmann, "The Significance of the Qumran Texts for Research into the Beginnings of Christianity," and Joseph A. Fitzmyer, "The Qumran Scrolls, the Ebionites, and their Literature," in *The Scrolls and the New Testament*, ed. by Krister Stendahl (New York, 1957); Hans-Joachim Schoeps, *Urgemeinde Judenchristentum Gnosis* (Tübingen, 1956). The literature on the Scrolls is voluminous. For further reading one should consult the writings of Allegro, Burrows, Brownlee, Cross, Dupont-Sommer, Rowley, etc., and the *Revue de Qumran*.

[8] Cf. The Book of Hymns I, 5-39, "Thou hast assigned the tasks of men's spirits duly."

[9] Gaster, *op. cit.*, p. 45.

[10] *The Manual of Discipline*, viii. 1-19.

the sense of expectancy arising from Pharisaic devotion to Torah, and the more intensive exhibition of high moral living of Essenes and Covenanters (if these were separate). All took seriously the demand to be God's elect. All were inescapably affected by political and economic unrest, especially in Galilee.[11]

II

John the Baptist came upon the scene preaching the necessity for repentance in preparation for the Kingdom of Heaven which was at hand (Matthew). The words from Isaiah were remembered, "the voice of one crying in the wilderness, prepare the way of the Lord."[12] Whether or not John's diet and dress were unusual,[13] the prophet separated himself from regular religious expression despite the fact that he was probably of priestly family. The urgency of his message pointed to the Judgment of God already imminent, even begun, and the coming of the Mightier One. In contrast to John's blazing message, the *Manual of Discipline* approaches the same goal in milder fashion: "Unclean, unclean he remains so long as he rejects the government of God and refuses the discipline of communion with him. . . . Only by a spirit of uprightness and humility can his sin be atoned. Only by submission of his soul to all the ordinances of God can his flesh be made clean." (ii, 25-iii, 12). John also demanded a righteous life as evidence of repentance. His disciples fasted (Mark 2:18) perhaps more than the Law required, but almost certainly as a symbol of repentance. Above all, John came "in the way of righteousness" (Matt. 21:32).

Just as John cannot be identified with any of the Jewish groups or sects, neither can Jesus. As far as we know, the only group to which Jesus attached himself for a time was that of John the Baptist. Jesus was no ascetic. He neither lived as John nor did he repudiate marriage. Independent of all groups, he rose above the turmoil of party and national politics.[14] Early in his career he was "set between two opposing realms, the divine and the Satanic."[15] The Kingdom of God (Heaven) was at hand, imminent, but to those who had

[11] Cf. Sherman E. Johnson, *Jesus in His Homeland* (New York, 1957).

[12] Cf. *The Manual of Discipline*, ix, 16-20, "For this is the time when the way is being prepared in the wilderness."

[13] Carl H. Kraeling, in *John the Baptist* (New York, 1951), thinks they were not; but why do Mark, Matthew and the Gospel of the Ebionites bother to mention them?

[14] Cf. Farmer, *op. cit.*, p. 191.

[15] T. W. Manson, *The Teaching of Jesus* (Cambridge, 1955), p. 196.

accepted it, present.[16] It was worth all it cost in comparison with the usual values of life. The saved would be few, the gate narrow and the way hard for those who found life. Although Jesus approved fasting (without making a display), his disciples did not fast and, in his words, "the Son of Man came eating and drinking." In the Parable of the Sower the cares of the world and the delight in riches choke the word. Later, the return of one hundred-fold is interpreted as the martyrs, the sixty-fold, the virgins. Following Jesus meant self-denial and possibly the renunciation of one's family. When, because of his position on divorce, the disciples replied, "it is not expedient to marry," Jesus seemed to agree, "Not all men can receive this precept, but only those to whom it is given" (Matt. 19:11). Matthew adds the verse describing three kinds of eunuchs: those from birth, those made so by men, and those who have made themselves eunuchs for the sake of the Kingdom of Heaven. But only he who can receive this may receive it. Nor is there any marrying in heaven. As the ascetic ideal attaches itself to early Christianity the celibate life is not for all, but only for those who can stand it, and this has been bestowed as a gift.

The rich young man, in order to be perfect, must sell what he has, give to the poor and follow Jesus. This he could not do, for he was very rich. Jesus does not hesitate to point out how hard it is for the wealthy to get into the Kingdom. The disciples, showing their astonishment, asked then who could be saved. Was the astonishment feigned and was the question sardonic? We have no reason to believe so. If the question was genuine we have additional light on what the disciples thought of salvation. Sirach, the Psalms of Solomon and Enoch note the disparity between rich and poor.[17] The rich are enemies of God and subject to "woes." Later, Clement of Alexandria will ask whether a rich man can be saved and will respond affirmatively if the wealthy man distributes his possessions among the less fortunate. Luke heightens the demands of the other Gospels.[18] The poor have the gospel preached to them. According to Luke it is the poor (*not* "in spirit," as in Matthew) who have the Kingdom, the hungry who will be satisfied, those who mourn who will be happy. All of these downtrodden and neglected can be happy now

[16] Manson, *op. cit.*, and Werner Georg Kümmel, *Promise and Fulfilment*, trans. by Dorothea M. Barton (Naperville, Ill., 1957).

[17] Ecclus. 5:1; 11:14, 19; 13:19, 24, etc.; Ps. Sol. 5:2, 13; 10:7; 5:2; En. 94:8; 96:4, 5.

[18] I am indebted here to my colleague, Professor Burton H. Throckmorton, Jr., "Jesus' view concerning his disciples' proper relation to the world," *The Alumni Bulletin*, Bangor Theological Seminary, XXXIV, No. 1 (Jan. 1959).

for their relief has already begun. But woe to the rich, the satiated, those who laugh now! Not even Moses and the prophets or some one risen from the dead can save the five brothers of the rich man from repeating his mistreatment of Lazarus, the poor man. It was the poor, maimed, blind and lame who were bidden to the banquet after those first invited had refused. The Kingdom and discipleship both made demands for renunciation, self-sacrifice and discipline.[19] Indeed, discipleship means renouncing everything (Luke 14:33).

As we have seen, Jesus on one occasion referred to John as one who came "in the way (ἐν ὁδῷ) of righteousness." Jesus had already commented upon the narrow way and the spacious way (Matt. 7:13, 14). It is no less striking that the same word, the Way, is used four times in Acts (9:2; 19:9, 23; 24:22) to designate the Christian movement. Later, the way of renunciation and righteousness became also, through the example of Jesus, the way of the cross. Renunciation, then, may lead to martyrdom.[20] But it is not merely a matter of "making a good end," but of taking up the cross *daily*. The Way, then, becomes the royal way of the cross. Later still, the doctrine of the Two Ways will be found in the *Doctrina Apostolorum*, the Didache, the Epistle of Barnabas and the Apostolic Constitutions.

III

We have little information concerning the first Christian church in Jerusalem. The apostles with some women formed the core of the group, which seems to have increased rapidly. Peter, the sons of Zebedee, and James emerged as leaders. The followers of the Way who saw the risen Jesus as God's Messiah worshipped in the temple, sold their property, holding all things in common, incurred the enmity of the Sadducees, but seem to have been championed by at least one Pharisee (Gamaliel). A great many priests even joined the group. The persecution which resulted after the martyrdom of Stephen strangely did not touch the apostles. That the theological interpretation of Christ and his mission (and even the pursuit of the Way) on the part of Jewish Christians in Jerusalem would differ from that of Gentile converts goes without saying. In the early decades of Christianity there was a Jewish strain and a Gentile strain. Acts and Paul's letters reflect tensions arising from the

[19] As T. W. Manson has shown, *op. cit.*, pp. 205 f.

[20] Marcel Viller, "La spiritualitè des premiers siécles chrétien," *Bibliothèque Catholique des Sciences Religieuses*, 32e. (1930), p. 7: "La souffrance et la persécution entrent pour une part dans la perfection. Instruments de mérite, elles ont une influence considérable sur l'autre vie : 'Bienheureux les pauvres. . . .' "

different emphases.[21] One has only to cite the parties at Corinth and the total ignoring of the founding of the church in Alexandria. In passing we should note that James, brother of Jesus and later head of the Jerusalem church, is said by Eusebius (reporting Hegesippus) to have been called "the Just" from the time of the Savior, and to have used no wine, to have eaten no meat and to have refrained from bathing, shaving and anointing with oil. It is striking that neither the Gospels nor the Acts mentions these matters.

Paul, thorough Jew of the Diaspora, mystic, individualist, apostle, fell under the spell of early Christian eschatology. But he had to deal with the problem of sin, personal and universal; in his flesh no good dwells.[22] "The mind that is set on the flesh cannot please God . . . and those who are in the flesh cannot please God" (Rom. 8:7, 8). If Paul has in mind here the two "inclinations,"[23] what becomes of the inclination for good and what happens to the belief that study of Torah overcomes the evil impulse? The main purpose the Law served was to reveal sin and he is helpless until Christ dwells in him. Who will deliver him from "this body of death?" God will, through Christ. Yet Paul is still in the flesh, not understanding his own actions, so he pummels his body and subdues it. This expression follows the reference to the athlete who exercises self-control (ἐγκρατεύεται, I Cor. 9:25; in 7:9, ἐγκρατεύονται). The Greek word from which we derive asceticism is ἄσκησις, meaning originally "exercise" or "training" such as an athlete undertook to prepare himself for the games. Luke uses the verb ἀσκέω (to exercise oneself) in reporting Paul's speech before Felix (Acts 24:16). From physical exercise the word acquired moral connotation, so that one disciplined his body in the interest of a higher life.[24] Does this not parallel Paul's thought? If the evil impulse so monopolizes the flesh as to destroy man, must he not discipline and subjugate his body so that Christ may come in?

---

[21] Cf. S. G. F. Brandon, *The Fall of Jerusalem and the Christian Church* (London, 1951).

[22] Cf. John A. T. Robinson, *The Body* (Chicago, 1952).

[23] So W. D. Davies suggests in *Paul and Rabbinic Judaism* (London, 1948). Davies also summarizes the position of H. Wheeler Robinson, *The Christian Doctrine of Man;* F. R. Tennant, *The Fall and Original Sin;* N. P. Williams, *The Ideas of the Fall and of Original Sin.*

[24] Edward Spranger and Romano Guardini, *Vom Stilleren Leben* (Würzburg 1956), pp. 32-33: "Der Trieb kommt aus seiner physisch-psychischen Quelle und sucht einfachhin Erfüllung; das sittliche Gebot aber tritt ihm entgegen. . . . So bedarf es schon hier einer Wachsamkeit, die feineren Stimmen zu hören; einer Übung, sie zu stärken und ihnen Führung zu gehen. Das ist dann bereits Askese."

Furthermore, closely associated with asceticism was the idea of merit. According to Davies, Paul sees the sacrifice of Christ as efficacious for others. Davies points out that "it was a postulate of Rabbinic thought that a man by his obedience to the Torah could obtain merit."[25] We have already seen that the Covenanters at Qumran believed that *their* righteous life could be efficacious for the whole earth. James says that "the prayer of a righteous man has great power in its effect" (5:16).

Goguel has remarked upon the lack of pneumatism in the church at Jerusalem in contrast to that found in Gentile Christianity.[26] Paul was conscious of what it meant to be filled by the Spirit and no less aware of his unique conversion experience. He also realized that God's appointed hour was near and that "the form of this world is passing away." It is under this tension that he makes his judgments concerning marriage. Marriage is good only as a preventive of immorality and nothing is said in favor of procreation. He wishes all could remain as he is, that is, unmarried, but recognizes that "each has his own special gift from God." If a person is unmarried let him stay that way "in view of the impending distress." Because time is short those who have wives ought to live as though they had none. The married are concerned with this world and each other; the unmarried can give themselves to the Lord.[27] Paul's meaning in 1 Cor. 7:36 f. is unclear, but probably the letter was written before the origin of the παρθένοι συνείσακτοι.[28] However, in regard to the problem of marriage there are two planes : marriage is permitted, it is no sin; but the higher plane is the unmarried, or if married, the continent, state. In later Judaism sin is traced to the woman, and one of the results of Adam's sin is the begetting of children.[29] Clement of Alexandria, in attacking heresy, reports from the heretical Gospel of the Egyptians the words of Jesus after Salome inquired how long death would have power, "As long as you women bear"; and later, Jesus says, "I came to destroy the works of the female."[30]

Paul also had to contend with the messenger of Satan, and more than once Satan had kept him from coming to the Thessalonians

---

[25] *Op. cit.*, p. 268.

[26] Maurice Goguel, *The Birth of Christianity*, trans. by H. C. Snape (New York, 1954), pp. 98 f.

[27] Cf. Karl Müller, *Die Forderung der Ehelosigkeit für alle Getauften in der alten Kirche* (Tübingen, 1927).

[28] Cf. Achelis, *Virgines subintroductae* (Leipzig, 1902); H. Koch, "Virgines Christi," *Texte u. Unters.*, I (Leipzig, 1907); M. Goguel, *op. cit.*

[29] Ecclus. 25:24; II Bar. 56:6.

[30] Johannes Quasten, *Patrology* (Westminster, Md., 1950), I, 113.

(I Thess. 2:18). Paul saw life as a battle ground between Satan and the demons on the one hand and Christ and the believer on the other.

Elsewhere I have shown how the Greco-Roman world of the first century of our era exhibited various practices arising from the ascetic ideal.[31] What was this ideal? To the philosopher, and this would include Philo, it meant the subjugating or disciplining of the body for the good of the soul, so that the latter could escape its prison house (Pythagoreanism, Platonism, Neo-Platonism). The odd actions of the Cynic who restricted his diet and possessions to bare necessities was probably more of a protest against the social and economic extravagances of society than a religious outburst. On the other hand, the goal of the Stoic was to accept life as the will of God, whatever came, and to be content with his lot. The goal of the philosopher was ἀπάθεια. In the mystery religions where union with deity was the objective, sexual intercourse and certain foods were prohibited at specified times to free the body of demonic control.[32]

IV

The Greco-Roman world, then, knew what renunciation, abstinence, self-denial and discipline of the body meant. It was also a demonic world in which righteous forces confronted evil powers. Later Judaism, with definitely ascetic groups, with its apocalytic and eschatological emphases, its teachings upon sin and good and evil inclinations and its belief in meritorious prayer (if not yet a doctrine of merits) made its own contributions. Early Christianity intensified this through its teaching of the Way of self-denial, its expectation of the Kingdom, and through the mystical, ecstatic example of Paul and his interpretation of the gospel.[33]

As time passed and the return of the Messiah was delayed, the Church began settling down in its environment. That some churches too readily did this is made clear by the letters in Revelation to the churches at Ephesus (which has abandoned its first love), Sardis (which has the name of being alive but is dead), and Laodicea

---

[31] *Environmental Factors in Christian History* (Chicago, 1939), Ch. ix.

[32] H. Strathmann, *Geschichte der frühchristlichen Askese* (Leipzig, 1914), p. 258: "Der Geschlechtsverkehr macht kultisch unrein, letzlich weil er dämonisch infiziert."

[33] Cf. J. Klausner, *From Jesus to Paul*, trans. by William F. Stinespring (New York, 1943), pp. 490 f. See also Johannes Weiss, *Earliest Christianity* (New York, 1959).

(which is neither hot nor cold but which has prospered and is wealthy). Persecution, out of which came Revelation and I Peter, intensified the expectancy of the Day of Judgment, although the area to which Hebrews was addressed had not known persecution yet. The one hundred forty-four thousand in Revelation "who have not defiled themselves with women" are celibate.[34] In another situation Christians are warned against "deceitful spirits and doctrines of demons" and liars who prohibit marriage and certain foods (I Tim.). Widows spend their time in prayer, but only those over sixty are to be cared for; young widows ought to marry, for some through wantonness have already followed Satan. Women are not to braid their hair nor to adorn themselves with gold, pearls, or costly dress. They are to keep silent, for it was Eve who was deceived and sinned, not Adam. James champions the poor and warns that those who love the world are enemies of God. In other writings there is the requirement that Christians keep themselves unspotted from the world, for they are sojourners in this life and their citizenship is in heaven. They are *in* the world but not *of* it, and their Lord had prayed that his disciples might be kept from the Evil One. The world to which the Evil One is closely attached is not to be loved. Indeed the three concupiscences are "the lust of the flesh," "the lust of the eyes" and "the pride of life" (I John 2:16).

One theme common to later New Testament writings is the evident inroads being made by heretical teachings. Some of the radically dualistic Gnostic sects would not admit that Christ came in the flesh (Cf. II John 1:7). It is not our purpose to investigate Gnosticism[35] but simply to point out that its thorough-going dualism led to various ascetic practices even more stringent than those of the orthodox and more regular Christian movement.[36] Meanwhile, Ignatius, whose fervor matches that of Paul, is aware of the danger to the Church but also counsels those who are continent not to boast. Already in his time virgins are being enrolled along with widows in the Church's care.[37]

First-century Christianity, then, exhibited certain emphases

[34] Cf. Müller, *op. cit.*, p. 13: "Sie sind nicht die ganze Christenheit, sondern einer auserwählte Schar, die Vorläufer der bald nachher so genannten Enthaltsamen, der Asketen und Jungfrauen."

[35] A recent book by Hans Jonas, *The Gnostic Religion* (Boston, 1958), gives an excellent selected bibliography and selections from some important Gnostic documents.

[36] Later, apocryphal Gospels and Acts will intensify ascetic strains. Cf. Hans Lietzmann, *The Founding of the Church Universal*, trans. by Bertram Lee Woolf (New York, 1938).

[37] To Polycarp 5:2; To the Smyrnaeans 13:1.

which would be formalized later into regular ascetic discipline. Christianity was, first of all, a Way, or *the* Way, not only "of the Lord" but, like that of the Covenanters of Qumran, a way of righteousness to witness to and effect God's will.[38] It was not for a few but for all. In contrast to Gnosticism, which was a path to blessedness *after* life, the Christian "Way" was a way *through* life, and through death. But according to the summons and example of the Lord himself the "Way" was one of daily self-sacrifice and self-denial. The neglected, the outcast, the poor who accepted the good news were especially benefited but, since nothing is impossible with God, even the rich could be saved.

Concerning the whole question of marriage there is, for those who can bear it or receive it, a more excellent way, which is in refraining from marriage. Spiritual fervor and the lively expectation of the return of the Messiah not only militated against the usual worldly life but summoned Christians to special religious observances.[39] In bringing his own special emphases to the Christian message, and in contrast to Judaic Christianity, Paul magnified the continuing and titanic struggle between the Christ-filled believer and the demonic world.

Although the eschatological hope was delayed it was never given up, and persecution served to intensify it. But as the expected return of Christ did not materialize and the Church settled down it also made an honored place for widows and virgins and continued to insist upon a disciplined way for its members. Thus the ascetic ideal was implanted in first-century Christianity. It was to flourish and become institutionalized in the centuries to follow.

[38] Cf. S. Vernon McCasland, "The Way," *JBL*, LXXVII (1958), 222-230.
[39] Cf. Marcel Viller, *op. cit.*, p. 27: "Ainsi au IIe et au IIIe siècles la plus grande partie de la littérature spirituelle se concentre autour de la virginité qui, immédiatement après le martyre, constitue la perfection." Cf. also Arthur Vööbus, *Celibacy, A Requirement for Admission to Baptism in the Early Syrian Church* (Stockholm, 1951). An Armenian document, *Srboyn Ephremi matenagrowthiwnkh*, originally written in Syriac (second or third century) reports that Christians abandon all to follow Christ. This "imitation of Christ" is called a "war." The συνείσακτοι are regarded as living a spiritual mode of life par excellence.

XI | *Kenneth Willis Clark*
DUKE UNIVERSITY

THE SINS OF
HERMAS

I

Recently a Christian leader undertook to answer the question, "What is a . . . bishop?" In his answer he stated, "He is not a 'holy man' in the accepted meaning of the term."[1] It may not be clear how the term is accepted today, but the disclaimer was obviously intended to disarm the common Christian reader; and yet the Christian historian and theologian is aware that from the beginning Christianity demanded holiness not only from official leaders but from every professing member.

The immediate background for this Christian demand in the first century is represented in the admonition of Ben Sira (Ecclus. 21:1): "My child, have you sinned? Sin so longer, and offer petition for your previous sins." The *Discipline Scroll* of Qumran (iii, 9-11) similarly enjoins the novitiate to "direct his steps so as to walk perfectly in all God's ways . . . Let him not swerve either to the right or to the left, nor transgress a single one of God's words."[2] Again, about the turn of the era, the Wisdom of Solomon (15:2 f.) confidently insists: "We will not sin, for we know that we are accounted yours. For to know you is perfect uprightness."

Such typical expressions in late Judaism remind us of the principle of perfectionism proclaimed by Jesus (Matt. 5:48): "You are to be perfect, as your heavenly Father is."[3] Paul habitually addressed the Christian believers throughout his correspondence as "saints"

---

[1] T. Otto Nall, *Together* (March, 1958), p. 13.

[2] Translation of G. Vermès, *Discoveries in the Judean Desert* (New York, 1956).

[3] Cf. also Luke 6:36. Quotations from the English New Testament follow the Revised Standard Version.

or "holy persons." [4] When we come to the generation of Hermas of Rome we find the Christian literature sprinkled with similar phrases. For example, in Hebrews : "Holy brothers, who share in a heavenly call . . . "(3:1);" . . . the love which you showed . . . in serving the saints" (6:10). And in I Peter (quoting Lev. 19:2) : "You shall be holy, for I am holy" (1:16); "You are a chosen race, a royal priesthood, a holy nation . . . " (2:9); "Whoever has suffered in the flesh has ceased from sin, so as to live for the rest of the time in the flesh no longer by human passions but by the will of God" (4:1 f.). Ignatius reminds the Ephesians (14:2), "No man who professes faith sins," and in I John it is repeatedly urged, "No one who abides in him sins; no one who sins has either seen him or known him" (3:6); "No one born of God commits sin . . . he cannot sin because he is born of God" (3:9); "We know that anyone born of God does not sin" (5:18).

These are familiar passages but they are here recalled or three reasons : first, because the ideal of the perfect life has disappeared from contemporary Christian society; second, because in the current theological fashion the emphasis on universal sin has eclipsed the ideal of the sinless life; and third, because the experience and message of Hermas can be understood only when we revive the sense of Christian perfection which prevailed in his day.

Hermas was indoctrinated in this belief, as he reports in Similitude V (1:5) where the Shepherd charges him, "Do nothing evil in your life . . . let no evil desire arise in your heart . . . refrain from every wicked act . . ." [5] In Vision IV (2:5) the Church has set the goal to "serve the Lord blamelessly for the rest of the days of your life." [6] Again, in the fourth Mandate (1:11) the Shepherd directs that "he who has sinned sin no more," and later in the same Mandate (3:1 f.) Hermas reveals such instruction also from others : "I have heard, sir, from some teachers that there is no second repentance beyond the one given when we went down into the water and received remission of our previous sins." Such teachers as Hermas refers to were in accord with the conviction of the author of Hebrews that "it is impossible to restore again to repentance those who have once been enlightened" (6:4); "For if we sin

<hr/>

[4] E.g. Rom. 1:7; I Cor. 1:2; II Cor. 1:1; Phil. 1:1; Col. 1:2; II Thess. 1:10; Philem. 5.

[5] Quotations from the Apostolic Fathers are based on the Loeb edition, ed. by K. Lake (London, and New York, 1913), with occasional and minor independent revision.

[6] Cf. also I Clem. 40:4.

deliberately after receiving the knowledge of the truth, there no longer remains a sacrifice for sins, but a fearful prospect of judgment" (10:26).[7] This teaching was confirmed by the Shepherd in reply: "You have heard correctly, for that is so. For he who has received remission of sin ought never to sin again but to live in purity." Once more, in Sim. IX (18:1 f.) the Shepherd pronounces, "He who has knowledge of God is bound no more to do wickedly but to do good . . . those who have knowledge of God . . . and do wickedly . . . shall die for ever."

Many have held that Hermas had little support in this stern doctrine, but actually it appears frequently in the literature, both canonical and apocryphal. That we should find in dialectic contrast the realistic recognition that Christians do sin, does not invalidate the evidence that salvation was understood to depend not upon a favorable balance in the "book of life" but upon a clean page. A life of purity was thought to be quite possible and was indeed expected. The contemporaries of Hermas are not given to "Pauline pessimism" or capitulation to moral failure.[8] Hermas, as a typical Christian sinner, is not typical of all Christians; rather, his condition of post-baptismal guilt presents a special problem that applies to some Christians but not to most. The ideal picture is drawn in Sim. IX (29) where the white mountain shelters "innocent babes . . . no evil enters their heart, nor have they known what wickedness is, but have ever remained in innocence . . . all the days of their lives." Some moderns explain that such a life of purity was a more reasonable expectation in a day when the *eschaton* was imminent, but the early Christian could have had no illusion that the sinless life was easy even for a limited time. Hermas himself was conscious of failure and stricken with terror when he exclaimed (Vis. I, 2:1): "If this sin is recorded against me, how shall I be saved?"

It is against such a background that Hermas developed his distressing sense of guilt. The particular sins charged against him constitute the subject of our inquiry here, but we can entertain no doubt that he was concerned about his guilt. In the subconscious state of his first vision, he reports, "I . . . knelt down and began to pray to the Lord and to confess my sins" (I, 5:3). Again, in Vis. III (1:5 f.), in a similar state, he records, "I knelt down and confessed my sins again to the Lord, as I had also done before. And she (the personified Church) came . . . and listened to me praying

---

[7] See also Mand. IV (3:6-7).

[8] Sim. IX (23:4) has the formal expression, "Man who is mortal and full of sin," which refers to the general condition of the unregenerate, who are called upon to emulate God in his mercy.

and confessing my sins to the Lord." The occasion of the third vision was more than a year after that of the first, and therefore these two reports would not alone reflect habitual preoccupation with his sense of guilt, but on the later occasion the Lady upbraids him for persisting on the subject of his sins. In Mand. IV (2:3) Hermas bluntly admits, "I am a sinner . . . my sins are many and various." In Sim. VII (1 f.) an instructive interchange takes place when Hermas asks the Shepherd of Repentance to dismiss from his home the Shepherd of Punishment who has been tormenting him excessively, but the Angel of Repentance responds, "You must be afflicted . . . your sins are many. . . . " This at least is clear, that Hermas the Christian, who had once been baptized and cleansed of sin, was now again charged with sin and personally confessed his renewed state of guilt. This "plot" to the story is expressed emphatically in Vis. I (2:4) : "It is an evil and mad purpose for a revered spirit and one already approved, if a man desire an evil deed, and especially if it be Hermas the temperate."

II

What specifically were the sins of Hermas? The answer to this is difficult because his own report is often inconsistent and confusing, but the attempt to find the answer may yield useful insights not only biographical but psychological and theological as well. First of all, in Vis. I, Hermas sees the admired Rhoda in heaven, who explains to him, "I was taken up to accuse you of your sins before the Lord." Here at the outset the term "sins" is plural and undefined, and furthermore she assures him that she has not as yet made any charges—and the apocalypse never again refers to this function of hers. Nevertheless, she informs Hermas, "God . . . is angry with you because you sinned against me." This he denies as a false charge, insisting that he always respected her as a sister, indeed even as a goddess,[9] and never went so far as to speak a suggestive word to her. This refutation she appears to accept as the truth, for she then shifts to an allegation of a wicked desire in the heart (her knowledge of which is not explained).[10] To this Hermas makes no response, although earlier in the reported vision he did refer to her as "that woman I had desired." However, in the actual encounter he had insisted that his only thought was innocent as he reflected

[9] Instead of "goddess," Codex A reads "daughter," and the Ethiopic reads "lady."

[10] Cf. Matt. 5:28, paralleled in the Talmud (e.g., Shabbath 64a and Berakoth 24a). Cf. Epictetus *Discourses* II.xviii.15.

in his heart how admirable her beauty and character as befitting a good wife. The possible psychological subleties here are elusive, and yet it may be that Hermas would have the reader understand that this was the basis of the charge of an evil design. Some have taken the episode to imply his psychological infidelity. When Rhoda asks if in a good man an evil desire is not equivalent to an evil deed, Hermas makes no response as she goes on to affirm that it is so.[11]

At a later moment he finds himself in the presence of the old woman who personifies the Church, when she insists with finality, " . . . the thought did enter your heart concerning her. It is such a design as this which brings sin on the servants of God" (2:4). But Hermas himself makes no confession on this point and admits no evil action or intent. Although Rhoda has as yet laid no charge before the Lord, nevertheless she declares that his sin against her is the cause of God's anger. When the vision has passed, the shaken Hermas is in despair, considering that this sin had been recorded against him; but to him it is a false allegation for which he admits no guilt and of which he has not been convicted, though he makes no further defense of his innocence and no remonstrance against being falsely charged.

But if we are to understand that Hermas was held guilty of the evil thought, it should be remembered that this sin must be of long standing. A long interval had elapsed during which Hermas married and had a grown family. Since his encounter with Rhoda at the river Tiber she had died, and "after some time" he saw her in a vision in heaven. The psychologist might ponder whether he first became aware of his attitude toward her when he served as her slave in younger years, or when "after many years" he courteously helped her from the river, or even later when she appeared in his first vision. In the light of this psychological perplexity, a nice point to clarify is whether this sinful thought *originated* before or after his baptism; if before, his sense of guilt must be associated with its continuance or recurrence in some post-baptismal time. It will be granted that Hermas was not concerned with such refinement of theory; nevertheless certain theological implications are present in the situation. At the last, Rhoda's very charge—expressed gently and without reproach—strikes him with surprise and incredulity. It is made to appear that only God knew of his subconscious and secret desire, even without any formal accusation by Rhoda. Consequently, this allegation does not explain any sense of guilt in Hermas himself, to satisfy the "plot" of the story. Before the first

[11] Cf. Matt. 5:27; Mand. XII (2:3); Epictetus *Diss.* II.xviii.15-19.

vision closes the Church denies that such a sin has made God angry with Hermas (3:1).

Another passage in Mand. IV (1:1 f.) also may have reference to the personal sin of Hermas, where the Shepherd instructs him, "Guard purity and let not any thought come into your heart about another man's wife, or about fornication or any such wicked thing; for by doing this you do great sin. But if you always remember your own wife you will never sin."[12] We are not told whether Rhoda, who had owned him as slave, had been married at any time, nor are we informed as to whether Hermas became married during or after his period of slavery. The Shepherd's Mandate does not fit exactly the biographical account of Hermas, but seems to be a general rule which developed out of his personal problem.[13] In the same fourth Mandate (1:4 f.) Hermas inquires of the Shepherd, "If a man have a wife faithful in the Lord, and he find her out in some adultery, does the husband sin if he lives with her?" We note that the wife is "faithful in the Lord," that is, a Christian; that the conversation discusses not her sin but only that of her Christian husband. Here the Shepherd propounds the principle, "So long as he is ignorant, he does not sin. . . . "[14]

This principle is but lightly affirmed in our document, as it appears obliquely in only two other places. In Sim. V (7:2 f.) the Shepherd declares the unity of flesh and spirit and denounces the belief that the flesh may be defiled with impunity. When Hermas points out that a man (perhaps himself?) may have acted in ignorance prior to the Shepherd's teaching, the latter concedes that God can forgive him. Again, in Sim. IX (18:1-2) the Shepherd instructs that knowledge of God makes a man all the more subject to his punishment. A contemporary apology, the Preaching of Peter (Frag. VIII),[15] gives similar comfort: "Whatsoever any of

[12] Cf. Exod. 20:17 and Deut. 5:21. Tertullian's slur upon Hermas was quite undeserved (*De Pudicitia* 10 and 20).

[13] A point of special interest emerges from the Shepherd's further words (Mand. IV,1:2): "For if this desire enter your heart you will sin." The clear meaning of the future verb is not that you do sin in the thought but rather that the evil thought is parent to the overt deed which is sin. The idea has a parallel in the teaching of Jesus that whereas hate may lead to killing, both the overt deed and the incipient thought are equally sinful. But there is the subtle implication in Hermas that the evil thought is sin not of itself but rather because it is potential of the overt sin. So also Vis. I (2:4), whereas both senses are present in Mand. IV (1:1).

[14] The same idea is expressed in positive form in Jas. 4:17.

[15] See Clem. Alex. *Strom.* vi.6,48; J. N. Reagan, *The Preaching of Peter* (Chicago, 1923).

you did in ignorance, not knowing God aright, if he, having learned to know, repent, all his sins will be forgiven him.'' Although these passages are similar in pointing out that ignorance makes a critical difference in the sight of God, it must be noted that they do not support the exact principle declared by the Shepherd in Mand. IV; for whereas they state that God is lenient to forgive a sin committed in ignorance, the Shepherd has said that the husband's ignorant conduct is not even to be counted as a sin. Furthermore, Sim. IX and the Preaching of Peter speak of general knowledge of God, whereas Sim. V and Mand. IV refer to explicit knowledge of fact. If the Shepherd's Mandate represents the position of Hermas, then the latter's ignorance of evil might make further claim to innocence in the case of Rhoda.

III

The next allegation of sin made against Hermas is expressed also in the first Vision. This time the charge is made by the Church in the person of the old woman. When he complains to her of Rhoda's accusation, she explains, "But it is not for this that God is angry with you, but to lead you to convert your family (οἶκος) which has sinned against the Lord, and against you, their parents." The modern reader may breathe a sigh of relief here in the interest of Hermas, because so slight a sin replaces one so heinous. A lack of domestic responsibility is not found among the sins commonly listed in the generation of Hermas. That it is here considered a sin is indicated by the transfer of God's imputed anger from the sin of evil desire to the sin of domestic negligence. Furthermore, we shall find that this new charge is equally serious, equally persistent throughout the document, and equally intricate in this apocalyptic report.

To placate God, Hermas is called upon to "convert" (ἐπιστρέφειν) his family or household. The English term "convert" conveys the thought that his family still are heathen and that he is to make them Christians. However, the context of the apocalypse shows that this is not the case, but rather that the reference is to the need for post-baptismal correction and reform. Their reform is the personalizing of the universal message of the book.[16] The household here referred to means only his own offspring, sons and daughters, called interchangeably ὁ οἶκος or τὰ τέκνα or occasionally τὸ σπέρμα.[17] In only three instances the double term "children and household" appears, as though Hermas' moral responsibility might extend more

[16] See Vis. I (1:9; II (2:4 f.).
[17] See Vis. I. (3:1-2); II (2:2).

widely.[18] His own children must have been numerous, since they are referred to as "all your children" (τοῖς τέκνοις σοῦ πᾶσιν, Vis. II, 2:3) or "all your household" (ὅλου τοῦ οἴκου σου, Vis. I, 1:9 and Sim. VII, 3 Latin). It would seem that these children are grown and morally responsible persons, who were previously converted to the Christian life as adults and have subsequently built up a shameful record of sinfulness.

Yet it is accounted as a sin of Hermas, engendering the wrath of the Lord against *him*, that his adult Christian offspring have sinned (ἀνομήσαντα, Vis. I, 3:1). The Church's accusation is: "You have not been instructing your family, and have allowed them to become terribly corrupt" (*Ibid.*). Their sin is said to be against the Lord and against the parents. What is meant by sinning against the parents is not made clear, and yet such an explanation is especially needed when we find no reference to the responsibility of the mother and only condemnation of the negligence of the father. Hermas is placed in the peculiar position of being responsible to God for sins committed against himself by his undisciplined children.

The nameless wife of Hermas plays only a minor part in the problem of his divine condemnation. She is mentioned only in Vis. II (2:3 f.) as his companion (σύμβιος) who sins with an uncontrolled tongue. It is not said whether this means gossip, grumbling, guile, abuse, or even blasphemy. Far too much has been imagined as to her bad character, despite the fact that the brief reference is really quite favorable to her. Hermas is to deliver the Church's message to all his children and his wife, and when she shall have heard it she will control her tongue and obtain mercy.[19] She is, however, quite unimportant to the "plot" and there is no explanation as to why Hermas is directed to consider her as a sister in the future. Perhaps we may judge from Mand. IV (4) that here also it is proposed to Hermas that he go beyond the normal requirement of morality.[20]

What are the sins of the children of Hermas, which fall upon the latter's shoulders? Two are specifically mentioned, double-minded-

---

[18] See Mand. XII (3:6); Sim. V (3:9); Sim. VII (6). Some have proposed that the term οἶκος here means the larger "flock" of Christians, but this is an improbable meaning for the synonyms τὰ τέκνα and τὸ σπέρμα.

[19] Codex Aleph here reads, " . . . you will obtain mercy."

[20] Mand. IV (4) contains the Shepherd's advice that remarriage is not a sin, and yet if the widower "remain single he gains . . . great glory with the Lord." Unlike Paul's objective (I Cor. 7:28 f.), it is here to "preserve purity and holiness." This idea of supererogatory conduct is mentioned again by Hermas in Sim. V (3:3): "If you do anything good, beyond the commandment of God, you will gain for yourself greater glory." See also 2:7 and 3:7 f.

ness and blasphemy, the latter of which should be considered fatal. They are mentioned in the general setting of persecution and apostasy (Vis. II, 2:2, 4, 7 f.).[21] Elsewhere it is implied that their sin is constituted of many daily evils which can be overcome only by "the daily righteous word" (ὁ λόγος ὁ καθημερινὸς ὁ δίκαιος), like the persistent strokes of the smith (Vis. I, 3:2). Although the sins of these Christian children may be many and varied and unidentified, the total result is fearfully impressive: "Your seed, Hermas, have offended God, and blasphemed the Lord, and through their great wickedness have betrayed their parents ... they have added to their sins (ἁμαρτίαις) licentious acts (ἀσελγείας) and a mass of iniquity (πονηρίας), and so their sins (ἀνομίαι) have been made complete" (Vis. II, 2:2). The psychologist would say today that Hermas must have been greatly concerned about the sins of his children, for this theme is repeated with emphasis in Vis. I and Vis. II, and again especially in Sim. VII (2 f.) where it is the "glorious angel"[22] (rather than God) who is "enraged at their deeds" of "great iniquity and sin," and yet the burden of guilt is laid upon Hermas as "the head of the whole household."

Despite their evil record, including blasphemy, the Church assures Hermas that "if they repent with all their heart, they will be inscribed in the books of life with the holy people" (Vis. I, 3:2). In Sim. VII (2) the Shepherd extends release to Hermas himself: "When, therefore, they repent, and have been purified, then the Angel of Punishment will depart from you." But the reader is perplexed when Hermas remonstrates (4), "They have repented with all their heart," and the Shepherd responds, "I already know that they have." Yet relief cannot come to Hermas immediately, he explains, because now the repentant ones must undergo affliction and self-imposed torture for a time.[23] In Vis. III (7:5 f.) the Church explains that the rejected "stones" may repent but they are less worthy even "after they have been tormented and fulfilled the days of their sins," i. e., a day's torment for a day's sin. Then when Hermas comments (Sim. VI, 4:2) that the penalty should be sevenfold, the Shepherd's explanation is that a single hour of torment has the "power" of thirty days, or one day the power of a year.[24]

[21] See Vis. III (7) for the double-minded "stones" in the tower allegory.

[22] Probably the same "glorious angel" referred to in Sim. IX (1:3), who sent the Shepherd to dwell with Hermas. In Vis. V (2) he is called the "most reverend angel."

[23] See also Mand. IV (2:2).

[24] One hour to a month means a ratio of 1 to 720, unless only twelve daylight hours are in mind. One day to a year means probably 1 to 360, assuming a pure lunar year.

The afflictions for sin are administered by another shepherd, the Angel of Punishment, and Hermas asks what the different punishments are. It is to be observed that although he is himself under the Angel of Punishment he has not experienced these afflictions. He is informed that such tortures are suffered in this life, and that they include losses, poverty, sickness, shiftlessness and failure, and insults by inferior persons. After these afflictions, men are turned over to the Angel of Repentance for instruction (Sim. VI, 3:4-6).[25]

In Sim. VII (4) the Shepherd says that it is the repentant children who must do penance and suffer affliction for their own sins.[26] But he has just declared (2) that the "glorious angel," enraged at their deeds, has required that Hermas be afflicted. Indeed, it is implied that it is *his* affliction that will bring about their repentance. Similarly, in Mand. XII (3:6), the salvation of his children and household is said to be dependent on *his* obedience to the mandates. Yet again, in Sim. VII (5), the Shepherd observes, "It is advantageous for you and for your house, to suffer affliction now," as though all must share the affliction. The "glorious angel" has directed (1) that Hermas be placed in the charge of the Shepherd of Punishment to be tested and afflicted although, so the Shepherd says (2), his own sins are "not so great as that [he] should be handed over to this angel." "You must be afflicted," says the Shepherd (1), because the "glorious angel" has ordered it so, but (6) "I will ask the Angel of Punishment to afflict you more lightly." Again, it is promised (6) that the affliction will last only a short time, after which he will be "restored" to his household.[27] In the light of so many inconsistent and even contradictory remarks, it is extremely difficult to secure any positive impression as to the real guilt of Hermas in the matter of his responsibility as head of the household.

It is therefore not surprising that Hermas himself should disregard the charge of guilt by proxy and challenge the Shepherd to reveal any personal charge. Even after all the story about Rhoda and the account of his evil children, Hermas still innocently inquires (Sim. VII, 1), "What have I done so wicked?" The Shepherd admits

[25] The series of afflictions is given in connection with the parable of the well-fed sheep committed to the Shepherd of Punishment. Perhaps, therefore, these afflictions should be understood as especially applicable to those who live in luxury.

[26] In Sim. X (2:4) the principle is stated, " . . . each one . . . is guilty of his own blood."

[27] Some have drawn a biographical datum from this statement, that Hermas was a prisoner under arrest, but the natural meaning is that he will be delivered from the charge of the Angel of Punishment. We must remember that the imagery throughout is visionary and symbolical.

that his sins would not justify committing him to the Angel of Punishment but reiterates that his family has been sinful. To this Hermas again protests (3), "Even if they have done such things . . . what have I done?" Apparently he has not been impressed by the explanation of the Church in his first Vision (3:1) : "Because of their sins and iniquities you have been corrupted in daily matters"; nor by her words in the second Vision (3:1) : "You neglected them and became entangled in their evil deeds."

A more direct allegation is reflected in her instruction to him in Vis. II (3:1) : "You are no longer to bear malice against your children . . . for malice produces death."[28] But when Hermas later asks in Sim. VII "What have I done?", the Shepherd seems to grant that there is no serious charge directly against Hermas himself, for he replies (3) : "They cannot be punished in any other way, than if you, the head of the house, be afflicted. For when you are afflicted, they also will necessarily be afflicted, but while you fare well, they cannot suffer any affliction." The Shepherd promises in Sim. VII (2) that repentance by his children will release him from the punishing angel. Furthermore, the Church has praised him (Vis. II, 3:2, in a phrase from Heb. 3:12) for not having fallen away from the living God, but remaining in simplicity and continence.[29] That Hermas has been constant in such virtues is again implied in Sim. VII (6) : "Only continue in your humility and service to the Lord with a pure heart." Charges of neglect and malice have been mentioned but not sustained, and certainly not explained; while the impression remains that his afflictions are vicarious. As in the case of Rhoda, so also in the case of his family responsibilities it becomes a difficult and intricate matter to place at his own door some explicit and personal sin, with consistent and persuasive evidence.

IV

A third possible accusation against Hermas educed by critics from his apocalypse is that his mind has been set on prosperity and luxury. It is true that much is said about the sin of the wealthy, and also true that Hermas himself is said to have been wealthy

---

[28] The malicious are represented by the cracked stones in the tower vision (Vis. III,6:3). Cf. Sim. IX (23:4) : the term μνησικακεῖν has often been translated "to bear a grudge" but this seems less suitable to the context than "to bear malice," called here a demonic "heresy." Malice as a moral attitude is considered one of the worst of sins (cf. Mand. VIII,3 f.).

[29] The virtues of simplicity and innocence are commended in Mand. II (1 and 7). In Vis. I (2:4) these virtues are attributed to Hermas by the Church.

formerly (Vis. III, 6:7). Although he is wealthy no longer,[30] his constant concern with the sins of business and riches clings to him so as to persuade some that this is part of his struggle with guilt. A prelude to this theme appears in the very first of the visions, and it is Rhoda herself who first sounds the note. When speaking of his evil designs, she seems to have him in mind as she points out that evil designs bring death and captivity, "especially to those who obtain this world for themselves and glory in their wealth" rather than in "the good things which are to come" (1:8).

The theme of wealth is emphasized in the vision of the tower (Vis. III, 6:5-7), where the round, white stones are Christians who have both faith and wealth but whose business interests which misguide them (ψυχαγαγῶν) cause them to apostatize under persecution.[31] Their only hope lies in renunciation of their wealth, lest they renounce their Lord. "This you must understand," says the Church, "from your own previous experience." One may question here whether Hermas' financial decline has been due to his acceptance of the principle of renunciation or to misfortune.[32] The advice of the Shepherd to Hermas in Sim. IV (5) is to "abstain from much business and you will do no sin. For those who do much business also sin much, being engrossed in their business, and serving their Lord in nothing." It is further suggested to him (7) that "if anyone be occupied with but a single business, he can serve the Lord also."[33] The Shepherd alludes to the lies told by Hermas in doing business (Mand. III, 5), and Hermas condemns himself (3) as one who never in all his life has spoken a true word. I have "always spoken deceitfully with all men."[34] The man preoccupied with business, says the Shepherd (Mand. V, 2:1-2), is especially susceptible to ill temper which subverts his tranquillity and out of nothing produces bitterness, "because of daily business or of food or of some trifle, or about some friend, or about giving or receiving."

When Hermas asks (Mand. VIII, 3 f.) what are the vices to

[30] We take the participle ἔχων in Sim. I (4) as expressing a general condition rather than as a statement of fact pertaining to Hermas.

[31] In Sim. VIII (8) the half-dry, half-green sticks represent "those who are concerned with business and do not cleave to the saints." Sim. VIII (9) also speaks of the faithful rich, represented by the sticks two-thirds dry, who chose to mingle with the heathen. Cf. also Mand. X (1:4-5); Sim. I (10).

[32] The principle of renunciation is repeated in Sim. IX (31:1-2). Some would understand that Hermas' property has been confiscated.

[33] Among the sins associated with acquisitiveness are also covetousness, robbery and theft (Mand. VIII,5).

[34] Furthermore, says Hermas naively, "I gave out that my lie was true." Besides, "men believed my word."

avoid, the Shepherd includes evil luxury and much eating and extravagance of wealth (πολυτελείας πλούτου) among "the wickedest of all in the life of men." In Mand. XII (2:1) the Shepherd ranks adultery as the primary lust, after which in second place comes "extravagance of wealth, and much needless food and drink, and many other foolish luxuries" which "bring the servants of God to death." There is a special shepherd, the Angel of Luxury and Deceit (Sim. VI, 2), who engenders evil desires that lead to death or corruption. Death comes to the worldly who have also blasphemed against the Lord,[35] but for the corrupt not guilty of blasphemy repentance is still possible.[36] The latter pass, in their restoration, from the Shepherd of Luxury to the Shepherd of Punishment and finally to the Shepherd of Repentance. Their punishment matches their sin, turning luxury into poverty and business losses. Estimated by the force they exert on one's experience, every day of luxury is balanced by a year of poverty (at least in the memory).[37]

Further, it is possible to interpret the Shepherd as speaking of degrees of wealth. Several times he uses the heightened term πολυτέλεια to describe extravagance of wealth and food,[38] and it is especially significant that this term is employed when speaking figuratively about the joy of spiritual wealth in righteousness.[39] It is not made clear whether all wealth, greater or less, is condemned, although it is explicit stated that limited business activity need not controvert the demands of the Christian life (Sim. IV, 7-8). Some guidance is given by the Church (Vis. III, 9:2-4) when she instructs, "Do not take for yourselves a superabundant share of what God has created, but give also a part to those who lack . . . lack of sharing is harmful to you who are rich, and do not share with the poor."[40] The Shepherd also directs (Sim. I, 6) that you must "make no further preparations for yourself beyond a sufficient competence." This context is one of inspiring description commending spiritual wealth acquired in the heavenly city. How much

---

[35] Cf. Jas. 2:5-7.

[36] A similar thought is expressed in Sim. IX (19), where hypocrites from the "bare mountain" fare better than the hopeless apostates and blasphemers from the "black mountain."

[37] Cf. Sim. VI (5:3). It appears paradoxical that morally poverty is preferable to wealth and yet poverty is considered punishment for the sin of wealth. Furthermore, poverty is at once both the punishment and the corrective for the evil of wealth.

[38] Mand. VI (2:5); VIII (3); XII (2:1).

[39] Sim. I (10-11).

[40] Cf. Did. 4:6-8; Sim. X (4:3).

of all this belongs to the personal experience of Hermas? Since he no longer indulges in luxuries, a degree of covetousness at most may persist. Yet he shows himself to be a man of sensitive conscience whose religious concern seems greater than his attention to business interests that fall within permissible limits. As to the evils of prosperity, he seems to stand outside as an onlooker inquiring into general principles that define the sinless life. It is certain that the general instructions in Sim. I (8 f.) are given in the plural : "Instead of lands purchase afflicted souls . . . look after widows and orphans."[41] "For this reason did the Master make you rich."

Thus we are prepared for the teaching of the parable of the elm and the vine (Sim. II). The moral is that they are necessary to one another, for the fruitless elm (the poor man) that supports the vine (the rich man) increases its yield and the fruitful vine thus bears also for the elm. This is a realistic recognition, at least, that we have with us always both poor and rich—if not an approval of such an economy. Yet the rich man is here assumed to be "poor as touching the Lord" and the poor man is "rich in intercession and confession."[42] The surprising conclusion is an uncommon beatitude (10) : "Blessed are those who have wealth, who understand that their riches derive from the Lord." So the Shepherd has come round to an approval of those who have wealth and faith, who do not neglect to use their wealth in charity (a neglect with which Hermas has not been charged). When finally we again recall that Hermas no longer possesses wealth (Vis. III, 6:7), any personal charge against him on this point seems very weak indeed.

V

Perhaps Hermas has committed the sin of double-mindedness or doubt. Such an attitude is certainly treated as a sin and is dealt with throughout the document.[43] The special homily on the subject is in Mand. IX, which begins with the urging of the Shepherd, "Remove from yourself doubt . . . for any man of doubt, unless he repent, shall hardly be saved." In this context doubt is the antithesis of faith and it defeats the Christian's petitions to God. Earlier a young man appears to Hermas in a vision (Vis. III, 10:9) and pointedly responds to him thus : "You are all made foolish by your doubt." He explains to him (11:2-3) that the Church had appeared

---

[41] Cf. Jas. 1:27.

[42] Cf. Jas. 2:5.

[43] I Clem. 11:2 and 23:2 f.; II Clem. 11:2,5 and 19:2 also allude to this evil.

as an old woman "because your [pl.] spirit is old . . . and has no power through your enervation and doubt . . . weakened by the occupations of this life." A further reference to the connection between his business and his doubt may be implied in the allegory of the sticks (Sim. VIII, 8-9), where the half-green sticks are those doubters "who are concerned with business and do not cleave to the saints." Again, in the allegory of the stones (Vis. III, 7:1), the stones that roll beyond the road into the rough ground are doubting converts who "leave their true road . . . and err and wander miserably." Indeed, in Mand. X (1:1), it is said that doubt is sister to grief and ill temper. [44]

Another allegory is that of the twelve mountains (Sim. IX, 21), the fourth of which bears many herbs whose tops are green but whose roots are dry. These signify the double-minded, who profess their faith but possess no lasting conviction. Double-mindedness is "of the devil," says the Shepherd (Mand. IX, 11), and is an "earthly spirit" without power, as opposed to the power of faith which is from the Lord above. False prophets victimize the doubter who consults them (Mand. XI, 1-2). Here again we must ask, to what extent do these generalizations refer to Hermas and his sense of sin? The Church (Vis. II, 2:4) has pointed to the double-mindedness of his children, but the Shepherd charges him squarely (Sim. VI, 1:2): "Why are you double-minded concerning the mandates?" This question seems to mean (1:4) that Hermas is not confident that he can obey the mandates and so avoid future sin. [45]

But the doubt that is most vividly pictured is that of wavering in the face of persecution. While traveling on the public road, Hermas hears the ominous admonition of the Shepherd (Vis. IV, 1:4) : "Do not be double-minded, Hermas." After he has encountered the gigantic beast and has safely passed by, he meets the Church, who now assures him (2:4): "You have escaped great tribulation through your faith, and because you were not double-minded" in the face of persecution. She had commended and assured him once before (Vis. II, 3:2) : "You are saved by not 'having broken away from the living God,'[46] and by your simplicity." In our document, simplicity ($\dot\alpha\pi\lambda\acute\sigma\tau\eta s$) is the antithesis of double-mindedness, and therefore to attribute simplicity to Hermas is to clear him of that sin as a temptation to apostasy. If Hermas was actually guilty of doubt, it must have been an attitude undefined and general. He

---

[44] In Mand. V (2:1), ill temper or bitterness ($\dot\sigma\xi\nu\chi\sigma\lambda\acute\iota\alpha$) is said to lead astray the vain and double-minded.

[45] Cf. Mand. XII (3:4-4:5).

[46] Cf. Heb. 3:12, which is also a reference to apostasy.

neither confesses nor affirms this sin, but on the contrary is praised for its opposing virtue.

Double-mindedness is for some the forerunner of apostasy and irrevocable condemnation. When the Church finishes reading to him (Vis. I, 4:2) she asks: "Did my reading please you?" Hermas replies, " . . . the first part was hard and difficult," and this is the part he has just described (3:3) as "frightful, such as a man cannot bear." The Lady declares that this "first part was for the heathen and the apostates."[47] So also in the third Vision (6:1) she explains that the broken stones cast far away from the tower are the hypocritical "sons of wickedness," having no salvation. Also, in the parable of the sheep (Sim. VI, 2:3), those that "you see joyful and skipping . . . have been torn away from God completely . . . "; in the parable of the sticks (Sim. VIII, 6:4), the wholly dry sticks are apostates and blasphemers; and in the parable of the twelve mountains (Sim. IX, 19:1), the black mountain yields apostates and blasphemers. Indeed, often in the apocalypse the critical evil that brings final condemnation is blasphemy. For the joyous, skipping sheep "there is no repentance of life because they have added to their sins and blasphemed against the name of God." The dry sticks are blasphemers who "have finally perished to God." As for Hermas, he is nowhere charged with the ultimate sin of apostasy and blasphemy. The Church has said to him (Vis. II, 2:2), "Your children . . . have blasphemed the Lord," and yet his offspring are not finally rejected. Hermas himself certainly goes no further than doubt, and his doubt is not uncertainty of faith but rather a wavering confidence in his ability to fulfill obediently the mandates of the Shepherd.

VI

The purpose of this exploration has not been to exonerate Hermas of sin. He explicitly confesses guilt, at least in a general manner. Our examination of the treatment given the dominant sins in the apocalypse, especially those sins which many have charged to Hermas, has had two objectives: to judge the extent to which Hermas has been personally involved, and to expose to view certain theological implications. This is really a study of the Christian life in one special family, in the formative generation at the beginning of the second century. The sins of immorality, materialism, doubt and apostasy were clearly the foremost sins of that time, not only in the Shepherd of Hermas but in all the contemporary

[47] Cf. Vis. II (1:8).

Christian literature. But on the basis of this apocalypse, it is difficult to fix these sins clearly and explicitly on Hermas. His role in the document is as a foil, against which to expound these sins to his fellow Christians. While the message emerges from his personal experience, the apocalypse does not succeed in making Hermas the personal example of the sinner. Furthermore, it does not succeed in any attempt at a clear explanation of these sins, or of their sure consequences. The general principle which Hermas would teach is quite clear, but the definition of that principle remains vague and inconsistent.

There remains the impression that Hermas was a historical figure, and there is still the picture of a representative Christian family with its moral problems in a time of undefined theology. But we may not be persuaded that Hermas personally experienced all the problems and all the major sins which are discussed. His personality in the document is a composite one, in which the sins of his contemporaries are compounded.

Finally, let us make a few theological observations. First, Hermas is concerned about the sinless life here and now. The purity of the Christian society eclipses the eschatological view. Second, Hermas sees remission of sin as dependent upon the Christian's conduct and attitude within society.[48] This leads T. F. Torrance to object that Hermas knows nothing of "justification by grace alone."[49] But this judgment overlooks the fact that Hermas is discussing post-baptismal guilt. Certainly Hermas would have been heretical if he had postulated a second act of God, to recover the failure of a first act of grace. In the particular problem of Hermas, it must be man (the believer-sinner) who will undertake to appropriate anew the divine grace which has been once received but forfeited. The problem of post-baptismal sin was new and unique with Christians of his own day, a theological problem encountered here for the first time within the young Christian movement. Therefore this new problem required a new answer rather than mere repetition of the first principle of justification through grace. The revelation of Hermas teaches a limited extension of God's grace, for it is concerned not with twice-born men but with thrice-born men.[50]

---

[48] Cf. Bar. 19:10.

[49] T. F. Torrance, *The Doctrine of Grace in the Apostolic Fathers* (Edinburgh, 1948), p. 118.

[50] It should not be overlooked that Tertullian's earlier view is similar to the revelation of Hermas. In *De Poenitentia* 7, he observes that baptized Christians should "know nothing of repentance, and require none of it"; yet God, "although the gate of forgiveness has been shut and fastened up with the bar of baptism, has permitted it still to stand somewhat open . . . but never more."

It has become usual to disparage Hermas as a theologian,[51] and certainly he is not systematic. Yet there is reason to contend that critics have failed to perceive the finesse with which he handles intricate and undefined theological problems in a formative day. We conclude that the biographical setting is authentic though the data are artificially compounded, that the visions are credible though they are sometimes inconsistent (as visions can well be), and that the theology is at once formative and sharply penetrating. Hermas personally is less sinful and more brilliant than critics have been wont to see.

[51] For example, Torrance repeats such an estimate in these words: "He was possessed of little Christian penetration, and certainly not much skill in the exposition. . . ."

XII | *Horst R. Moehring*
BROWN UNIVERSITY

JOSEPHUS ON THE MARRIAGE CUSTOMS OF THE ESSENES

Jewish War II:119-166
and Antiquities XVIII:11-25

A study of Christian origins cannot take place *in vacuo*. Christianity arose in the eastern Mediterranean world, a world which was characterized to a very high degree by two cultures which at several points overlapped : Hellenistic and Jewish-Hellenistic. This syncretistic culture was more than the background of Christianity; it was the soil upon which it grew.[1]

Among our most important sources for the study of Hellenistic Judaism are the writings of Flavius Josephus (A.D. 37/8—c.100). For many centuries the narratives of Josephus were taken at their face value, and it has been only in more recent generations that scholars have exercised their critical faculties on these books. Besides textual studies,[2] source criticism soon began to occupy the center of attention. Although students disagree on many details, it is generally recognized that Josephus' main source in the later parts of his works is Nicolas of Damascus, court historian and secretary of Herod the Great. Besides Nicolas, many other sources have been either identified or postulated. Thackeray's detailed work on Josephus' style led him to the theory that only very little of the present text can be ascribed to Josephus himself, most of it being the work of several assistants.[3] The picture thus presented

---

[1] F. C. Grant, *Ancient Judaism and the New Testament* (New York, 1959).

[2] *Flavii Josephi Opera*, ed. B. Niese (7 vols., 2nd ed., Berlin, 1955).

[3] H. St. J. Thackeray, *Josephus, the Man and the Historian* (New York, 1929); cf. *The Works of Josephus* (Loeb Classical Library), of which Thackery edited vols. I-IV (London & Cambridge, 1926-30); *A Lexicon to Josephus* (Paris, 1930—).

was chaotic; Josephus, the great historian, had disappeared and left behind only scattered fragments of dubious reliability.

A fresh approach was first attempted by the Giessen historian, Richard Laqueur, who claimed that different points of view expressed in the writings of Josephus indicate a change of outlook on the part of the author, not necessarily a change in the source material used.[4] It was Martin Braun who first placed Josephus into the general framework of Hellenistic literature of the first century after Christ. His work was mainly concerned with Josephus' paraphrase or, as the author himself calls it, translation, of the biblical history. Braun showed how Josephus sometimes departs considerably from his Old Testament source and introduces novelistic elements into his narrative which are frequently erotic in character.[5] G. Delling has attempted to show that throughout the writings of Josephus the treatment of miracles follows a similar pattern, indicating the hand of one author.[6]

With the discovery of the Qumran material the study of Josephus received a new impetus, particularly during the discussion of the nature of the Essene sect.[7] But this new interest in Josephus makes it all the more mandatory that the study of his writings should make use of all possible tools of scholarship. Whether Josephus be used as a yardstick by which to measure the Qumran writings or vice versa,[8] no clear picture can be drawn unless a careful textual and form-critical study underlies every investigation.

Josephus wrote primarily for Gentile readers and his main purpose was to compose an *apologia pro vita sua et pro populo suo*. This may also explain the presence of classical allusions in his writings. Although the *Jewish War* has some allusions to classical authors, it does not try to imitate any particular classical model. Both the *Jewish War* and the *Antiquities* show evidence of familiarity with the same passages in Thucydides.[9] In the *Antiquities*, however, allusions to, direct quotations from, or imitations of classical authors, and

[4] R. Laqueur, *Der jüdische Historiker Flavius Josephus* (Giessen, 1920).

[5] M. Braun, *Griechischer Roman und hellenistische Geschichtschreibung* ("Frankfurter Studien zur Religion und Kulter der Antike," vol. 6, Frankfurt/Main, 1934); *History and Romance in Graeco-Oriental Literature* (Oxford, 1938).

[6] G. Delling, "Josephus und das Wunderbare," *Novum Testamentum* II (1958), 291-309.

[7] A. Dupont-Sommer, "On a Passage of Josephus Relating to the Essenes," *Journal of Semitic Studies* I (1956), 361-366; J. Strugnell, "Flavius Josephus and the Essenes: *Antiquities* xviii. 18-22," *JBL* LXXVII (1958), 106-115.

[8] B. J. Roberts, "The Qumran Scrolls and the Essenes," *NTS* III (1956), 58.

[9] Both the expression κρύφα ἀπέπεμψεν (*War* i.178) and the phrase τῷ δὲ λόγῳ ἀπέδρασαν αὐτόν (*Ant.* xiv. 103) are taken from Thucydides *Hist.* i. 128.

especially Thucydides, are so common that Thackeray has been led to name one of the συνεργοί mentioned by Josephus,[10] whose mannerisms are especially obvious in books xv-xix of the *Antiquities*, the "Thucydidean hack."[11]

The use of different sources, both named and unnamed, the employment of assistants, and the possible interpolation of the text on the part of Christian apologists, all make it very difficult to reach a definite conclusion as to which parts of the writings of Josephus are actually from his pen. It will be necessary to develop criteria by means of which such an identification becomes possible. We have referred to Delling's attempt to do this through his study of the treatment of miracles. A more thorough and significant investigation was made by Braun, who found that Josephus frequently introduces novelistic elements of an erotic character into passages where his sources are known to be free of such traits; Braun's study has shown, furthermore, that these erotic-novelistic elements are present in passages which, according to Thackeray, are the work of one or the other of his assistants. It would be possible to draw from this the obvious conclusion that the novelistic element must be the work of the one person who exerted his influence upon the entire work, namely Josephus himself. And certainly this conclusion would be valid if the insertion of novelistic-erotic passages into larger historical works had been a rare or unusual literary device during the late Hellenistic era. This, however, was not the case.[12] If, then, the use of novelistic elements was common in this period, even a writer of such poor stylistic abilities as Thackeray has shown the "Thucydidean hack" to be, would be able to make use of them. If it could be shown that this man, by the consensus of most Josephus students the least talented of the assistants, could and indeed did introduce such features, then it would be impossible to assign the novelistic passages throughout Josephus to any one orator, since his assistants could have used this literary device as well. If, on the other hand, it could be shown that the so-called hack was not sufficiently interested in erotic-novelistic elements to use them whenever he found them in his sources, then it could be reasonably argued that it was Josephus himself who was responsible for these passages and, consequently, had a greater share in the writings of his works than some of the older source-critical studies would indicate.

---

[10] *Apion* i. 50.
[11] *Josephus*, p. 110.
[12] Cf. particularly the treatment which Livy gives the suppression of the Bacchic cult in 186 B.C. : *Ab urbe condita* xxxix. 8-20.

Any comparative study of literary material must, if it is to yield acceptable results, be based on some sections which in both content and length allow comparison, either through similarity or through contrast. The writings of Josephus frequently cover the same material twice in different books. This is true of the early history of the Jews, their Law, and the life of Herod the Great. A part of the discussion of the Jewish nation and their customs and institutions is the account of the several sects found among the Jews, which also is found in two versions. The earlier and by far the longer account is given in *Jewish War* ii. 119-166, the second one in *Antiquities* xviii. 11-25, where a direct reference is made to the earlier description :

καὶ τυγχάνει μέντοι περὶ αὐτῶν ἡμῖν εἰρημένα ἐν τῇ δευτέρα βίβλῳ τοῦ 'Ιουδαϊκοῦ πολέμου, μνησθήσομαι δ' ὅμως καὶ νῦν αὐτῶν ἐπ' ὀλίγον.[13]
It seems safe to assume that the second account is based on the first, and that the person who composed it had the earlier section before him. His task, according to the reference, was to summarize the former account for those readers of the *Antiquities* who had not read the *Jewish War*.

According to Josephus himself,[14] he had the help of literary assistants in the composition of the Greek version of the *Jewish War*, although so thorough and careful a student of style as Thackeray was not able to distinguish the hands of the several assistants.[15] He characterizes their influence upon the work with these words :

> At any rate the immense debt which the author of the *Jewish War* owes to these admirable assistants is apparent on almost every page. Among other excellencies, the work contains a large and choice vocabulary—not confined to military terms—peculiar to itself, or but rarely represented in certain parts of the *Antiquities*.[16]

As long as the Semitic original of the *Jewish War* remains unknown, it is difficult to determine the exact amount of help which the assistants rendered Josephus in this work. If, as seems probable, in the *War* their task was mainly to transfer the Semitic original into correct Greek, the contents of the work are, for the most part at any rate, the responsibility of Josephus himself. It is to be noted that the work of the assistants differed in the *War* from that in the *Antiquities*. In the former the collaborators had before them a complete work which the author had already published, while in the

[13] *Ant.* xviii. 11.
[14] *Life* 338.
[15] *Josephus*, p. 106.
[16] *Ibid.*, p. 105.

latter this was not the case; here they seem to have had more freedom. The account in the *War* fully justifies Thackeray's verdict upon the literary abilities of the assistants employed in the preparation of the Greek edition. The style is elegant, the narrative interesting and smooth. The reference to the Greek concept of the Isles of the Blessed[17] seems to be an allusion to Hesiod.[18]

The main attention in the account of the Jewish sects is given to the Essenes, whose customs, rules, teachings, and way of life evidently made them the most interesting. Their discipline and simplicity of life are emphasized and discussed in great detail. For the particular interest of this study it is worth noting that the author mentions twice their views and rules concerning marriage. In both instances the text becomes rather detailed : οὗτοι τὰς μὲν ἡδονὰς ὡς κακίαν ἀποστρέφονται, τὴν δὲ ἐγκράτειαν καὶ τὸ μὴ τοῖς πάθεσιν ὑποπίπτειν ἀρετὴν ὑπολαμβάνουσιν. καὶ γάμου μὲν παρ' αὐτοῖς ὑπεροψία, τοὺς δ' ἀλλοτρίους παίδας ἐκλαμβάνοντες ἀπαλοὺς ἔτι πρὸς τὰ μαθήματα συγγενεῖς ἡγοῦνται καὶ τοῖς ἤθεσιν αὐτῶν ἐντυποῦσι, τὸν μὲν γάμον καὶ τὴν ἐξ αὐτοῦ διαδοχὴν οὐκ ἀναιροῦντες. τὰς δὲ τῶν γυναικῶν ἀσελγείας φυλαττόμενοι καὶ μηδεμίαν τηρεῖν πεπεισμένοι τὴν πρὸς ἕνα πίστιν.[19]

The second passage[20] discusses a schismatic group of Essenes who differed with the main body in their views on marriage. In spite of a textual difficulty,[21] it seems clear that these people contracted marriage for the sole purpose of securing offspring. The women are subject to a period of probation, and no intercourse takes place during pregnancy : ἐνδεικνύμενοι τὸ μὴ δι' ἡδονὴν ἀλλὰ τέκνων χρείαν γαμεῖν. The section ends with the statement that in the bath the women wear a dress, the men a loin-cloth.[22]

It is true that these two sections are not complete *novellae;* indeed, they are hardly novelistic in character; the author merely gives some information concerning certain groups of people. But it cannot be denied that this interest in the sexual habits of a religious

[17] *War* ii. 150.
[18] *Works and Days* 170 ff.
[19] *War* ii. 120-121. Could this, in part, reflect Josephus' personal experience? He was married at least three times; he was deserted by one wife and himself divorced another. *Life* 415, 426 f.
[20] *War* ii. 160 f.
[21] The ἐπειδὰν τρὶς καθαρσῶσιν εἰς πεῖραν τοῦ δύνασθαι τίκτειν hardly makes sense; the Latin has *constanti purgatione.*
[22] An information which may seem unimportant but was significant, because it indicated a divergence from the Greek habit and would, therefore, be of interest to Gentile readers.

community indicates that the author thought this particular aspect of their life important enough to be included in his narrative. It is this same attitude of mind which would induce the author to introduce erotic-novelistic elements into his narrative whenever its general character made this at all possible. This was frequently done in cases where the sources, such as the Old Testament, are still available and can be shown to be free of this trait at the passage concerned. It is evident, then, that at least one of the persons working on the writings of Josephus had a strong interest in this aspect of life and introduced references to it whenever possible.

The account of the Jewish sects in the *Antiquities* can be shown to be from the pen of the "Thucydidean hack." Besides the Thucydidean spelling of πράσσειν,[23] ἐλασσόνως,[24] ἐς,[25] the passage contains the form ὁπόσα,[26] which Thackeray[27] has shown to be typical for the style of this assistant.

The explicit reference to the passage in the *Jewish War* at the beginning of the account in the *Antiquities* makes it almost certain that the "hack" had this at his disposal when he wrote his version. It should be possible, through a comparison of the two passages with specific reference to the erotic elements, to get an insight into the working habits of this man. Such a comparison of the two sections leads to the following significant results.

The introductory paragraph in the *War* mentions the sects in this order: Pharisees, Sadducees, Essenes,[28] while the *Antiquities* cite them in the sequence, Essenes, Sadducees, Pharisees.[29] The latter work follows the sequence of the introduction of the *War* in its actual discussion of the groups, while the text of the *War* treats them in the order Essenes, Pharisees, Sadducees.

The amount of space given to the discussion of the individual sects varies in both instances and seems to indicate a shift of interest. The following table gives the number of paragraphs devoted to each of the sects, together with their respective percentages of the whole narrative.

[23] *Ant.* xviii. 13,17,20.
[24] *Ant.* xviii. 24.
[25] *Ant.* xviii. 19,21.
[26] *Ant.* xviii. 15.
[27] *Josephus, the Man and the Historian*, p. 112.
[28] *War* ii. 119.
[29] *Ant.* xviii. 11.

	Jewish War	Antiquities
Number of sections		
Essenes	42	5
Pharisees	2	4
Sadducees	3	2
	47	11
Percent of sections		
Essenes	89.36	45.46
Pharisees	4.26	36.36
Sadducees	6.38	18.18
	100.00	100.00

In comparing the respective lengths of the several accounts in the *Antiquities* with those in the *War*, the following percentage figures of increase or decrease respectively, are gained:

Essenes	-43.91%
Pharisees	$+32.10\%$
Sadducees	$+11.80\%$

It is obvious, from this statistical statement, that to the author of the section on the Jewish sects in the *Antiquities* the Essenes are of far less relative importance than to Josephus himself, who was the actual author of the *War*.

One might argue that the reason for this was a possible lack of interest in the Essene sect, their teachings and customs on the part of the audience for which the *Antiquities* were primarily intended. But this will hardly have been the case. It was the habit of Josephus to make specific comparisons with Greek or Roman beliefs and habits whenever possible, in order to illustrate the character of the Jewish people to the Gentile readers. In the *War* we find specific mention of the doctrine of the immortality of the soul with a reference to the Greek concept of the Isles of the Blessed,[30] indicating that the Essenes, just as the other sects, had some points in common with the rest of civilized mankind.

And yet the radical curtailment of the space allotted the Essenes in the *Antiquities* appears to be significant if one remembers that it is the account of this sect in the *War* which exhibits such a strong interest in the sexual habits of its members. If the "Thucydidean hack" had been particularly interested in this aspect, he would have incorporated these sections into his own account in the *Antiquities*. However, it is especially this part of the earlier narrative which is most radically abridged. The two long paragraphs in the

[30] *War* ii. 155.

War, mentioned above, are reduced to one part of one sentence: καὶ οὔτε γαμετὰς εἰσάγονται οὔτε δούλων ἐπιτηδεύουσιν κτῆσιν, τὸ μὲν ἐς ἀδικίαν φέρειν ὑπειληφότες, τὸ δὲ στάσεως ἐνδιδόναι ποίησιν, κτλ.[31] The work of the "Thucydidean hack" in this section, then, consisted of a radical abridgment of the original account of the *War*, including the elimination of all erotic elements, and the introduction of the mannerisms peculiar to his style. It can hardly be said that this activity of his has made the account any clearer to the modern student. Such a grammatically difficult construction as paragraph 19 has brought forth numerous attempts to explain what exactly the text says concerning the sacrifices of the Essenes, so far without any convincing success.[32]

Perhaps it is possible to summarize the conclusions under two points:

1) It appears legitimate to say that a man who eliminates erotic elements in his reproduction of source material which contains them is very unlikely to be responsible for the introduction of such elements into narratives the sources of which lacked them. This would indicate that it was, indeed, Josephus himself who had a strong interest in this particular aspect of human life, or, at any rate, introduced it into his writings.

2) But once it is clear that Josephus has a predilection for this material, the student ought to be careful to avoid taking such passages at face value. We may frequently be confronted with material introduced for literary purposes rather than with an account of facts. Furthermore, every use of Josephus for the study of the Judaism of his time must be based upon a careful analysis of his sources and the employment of his assistants. Although Thackeray may be overstating the case when he says that in Books xv to xix the assistants "have, it seems, practically taken over the entire task,"[33] one must keep in mind that assistants employed in Rome for stylistic reasons cannot necessarily be supposed to be experts on Judaism.

Under these circumstances it becomes all the more necessary to emphasize the canon laid down by Roberts: "The scrolls now become the yardstick by which Philo and Josephus are measured."[34] In the last analysis, this becomes a matter of paying more attention to a primary source than to a secondary, although ancient, one.

---

[31] *Ant.* xviii. 21.
[32] Cf. Strugnell, *op. cit.*
[33] *Josephus*, p. xv.
[34] *Op. cit.*

THE ORIGIN OF
TEXTTYPES OF
NEW TESTAMENT
MANUSCRIPTS

Recent finds of extensive early manuscript copies of New Testament books have made significant study of this topic possible. The Chester Beatty Papyri and the Bodmer Papyri—to mention no others— take us at least a full century closer to the originals than the previous oldest copies did. The Beatty Gospels (P^{45}), the Beatty Paul (P^{46}), the Beatty Apocalypse (P^{47}) and the Bodmer John (P^{66}), while not complete, are extensive enough to establish the texttype they represent for these parts of the New Testament.[1] In date they are close together—all but one in the early part of the third century, which is a long distance ahead of the great parchment codices, Sinaiticus and Vaticanus, from the fourth century.

These four documents have revolutionized our understanding of the early history of the manuscript tradition of the Greek New Testament. Present day concepts of the great texttypes differ markedly from those held before the publication and study of these documents. The words "Caesarean," "Alexandrian," "Western,"— and even "Byzantine" or "Syrian"—have changed their significance as labels for groups of manuscripts in the last twenty-five years.

But before we turn to a study of these changes, a clarification of terminology is essential as preface.[2] By texttype I mean the largest

---

[1] Frederic G. Kenyon, *The Chester Beatty Biblical Papyri: Description and Texts of Twelve Manuscripts on Papyrus of the Greek Bible* (London, 1933); Victor Martin, *Papyrus Bodmer II* (Geneva, 1956 and Supplement 1958).

[2] See my discussion of terminology in "The Significance of Grouping of New Testament Manuscripts," *NTS*, IV (1958), 73-92.

identifiable group of related New Testament manuscripts. This is the category familiar under Westcott and Hort's labels as "Neutral," "Alexandrian," "Western," and "Syrian." It is easily distinguished from the "family," the smallest and most intimately related group— a group whose inter-relationships are so close that its stemma or family-tree can be established with exactness. While the members of a family come from a short span of time and a specific place, the members of a texttype scatter over the centuries and the continents. Nor does the contrast end there. A family is *one* group : e.g., section *a* of the Ferrar Group (fam. 13a), but a texttype may be composed of tribes (like the Ferrar Group as a whole) and of sub-texttypes (like the two main divisions of the so-called "Caesarean" texttype).

The caution is necessary that attribution of a specific manuscript or Church Father to one of these texttypes has often been hastily and carelessly done. In a recent article, I have argued that three steps are necessary to the accurate establishment of relationship : (1) establishing agreement where the evidence splits three or more ways; (2) establishing agreement in readings peculiar to the texttype; (3) establishing agreement in a large majority of the total number of readings where variation exists. The first of these steps is a labor-saving direction finder; it rapidly points to the area of major relationship. The second is the essential demonstration of a significant amount of agreement in the distinctive features of the type. The third is the confirmation of relationship by quantitative demonstration, without which other tests often mislead the student.[3]

When we turn to the statements of the handbooks on texttypes we find them usually dated as to origin in the end of the third or in the fourth century, and their "making" is usually associated with specific Fathers : Lucian, Hesychius, and Origen. J. L. Hug made this connection in the early nineteenth century, and a dozen others have done likewise.[4] Leo Vaganay in his fine manual repeats this tradition, and usually treats the texttypes as the work of an individual.[5] The one big exception is the "Western Text" which he does

---

[3] "Method in Locating a Newly-Discovered Manuscript within the Manuscript Tradition of the Greek New Testament." *Studia Evangelica, Texte u. Unters.* 73 (Berlin, 1959), 757-777. Further studies have demonstrated the value of this third step in the demonstration of relationship, and have made possible a refinement of method which I hope to publish soon.

[4] J. L. Hug in *Einleitung in die Schriften des Neuen Testaments*, summarized by L. Vaganay, *Introduction to the Textual Criticism of the New Testament* (Eng. trans., London, 1937), p. 162.

[5] *Ibid.* p. 115, "The Egyptian or Hesychius' Recension" (4th Century), p. 112; "Lucian's Recension" (4th Century), p. 113; "The Palestinian or

not attribute to an individual, and which he characterizes as universal, ancient, and lacking in homogeneity. Can this legitimately be called a texttype? On page 118, Vaganay inclines to differentiate this "Western Text" from the great Greek recensions and the somewhat later Vulgate versions.

But Vaganay, somewhat inconsistently, elsewhere (pp. 101 and 113) supposes "the first systematic revisions to have been made in the second century." He bases this directly on a statement by Origen :

> Nowadays, as is evident, there is a great diversity between the various manuscripts, either through the negligence of certain copyists, or the perverse audacity shown by some in correcting the text, or through the fault of those who, playing the part of correctors, lengthen or shorten it as they please (*In Matth. tom.* xv, 14; *P.G.* xiii. 1293).[6]

Vaganay elsewhere treats the making of the Hesychian or Alexandrian revision as a process, and he is led to this by his discussion of P[45] in John and Luke.[7]

It must be noted, however, that different scholars exempt a specific texttype from a date-of-origin. Hort's assumption (now held to be invalid) that the Neutral texttype was an unedited preservation of the original placed its origin at the beginning. The counterblast of early twentieth-century champions of the Western texttype claimed it to be primitive and unedited, hence as "original" in date as Hort's claim made the Neutral. Everyone has since the days of Hort admitted the existence of a date-of-origin for his Syrian text, also called the Byzantine texttype or the *Koine.*

The first action required by the new evidence is to split the fourth-century date for the origin of the texttypes in half and to push the halves apart.

All the texttypes *began* earlier than we had assumed. The Bodmer John is essentially a witness to the Beta texttype (Hort's "Neutral"), but it is far from identical with the consensus of the later witnesses to this texttype.

But the Bodmer John (P[66]) is also a witness to the early existence of many of the readings found in the Alpha texttype (Hort's "Syrian"). Strangely enough to our previous ideas, the contemporary corrections in that papyrus frequently change an Alpha-type

---

Pamphilus Recension," possibly "the edition, more or less retouched of Origen's Palestinian text."

[6] *Ibid.*, p. 101.

[7] *Ibid.*, p. 119.

reading to a Beta-type reading (Hort's "Neutral"). This indicates that at this early period readings of both kinds were known, and the Beta-type were supplanting the Alpha-type—at least as far as this witness is concerned.

These same points had been noted by Gunther Zuntz in his magnificent study of the text of the Epistles. He located P^{46} with B 1739 sah boh Clem Orig as "proto-Alexandrian."[8]

He says,

> The Alexandrian work in the text of the Scriptures (in the Epistles) was a long process rather than a single act. Its beginnings were inconspicuous, and roughly 150 years passed before it culminated in the "Euthalian" edition. Prior to this final achievement, the Alexandrian correctors strove, in ever repeated efforts, to keep the text current in their sphere free from the many faults that had infected it in the previous period and which tended to crop up again even after they had been obelized. These labours must time and again have been checked by persecutions and the confiscation of Christian books, and counteracted by the continuing currency of manuscripts of the older type. None the less they resulted in the emergence of a type of text (as distinct from a definite edition) which served as a norm for the correctors in provincial Egyptian scriptoria. The final result was the survival of a text far superior to that of the second century, even though the revisers, being fallible humans, rejected some of its correct readings and introduced some faults of their own.

He would put P^{46} nearer the beginning than the end of this process. He locates the publication of the Pauline Corpus in Alexandria about A.D. 100; and argues cogently that "in the latter half of the second century the Alexandrian bishopric possessed a scriptorium, which by its output set the standard for the Alexandrian type of Biblical manuscript."[9]

Zuntz also found P^{46} a witness for the existence of Byzantine (our Alpha type) readings in the second century. His statement deserves full quotation :

> "A number of Byzantine readings, most of them genuine, which previously were discarded as 'late', are anticipated by P^{46}.[10] Our inquiry has confirmed what was anyhow

---

[8] Gunther Zuntz, *The Text of the Epistles* (Oxford, 1953), p. 156.
[9] *Ibid.*, pp. 271-273.
[10] The same is true of the sister-manuscript P^{45}; see, for example, Matt. xxvi.

probable enough : the Byzantines did not hit upon these readings by conjecture or independent error. They reproduced an older tradition. The existence of this tradition was in several cases borne out by some versions or patristic quotations; but where such evidence is not forthcoming, the inference proved no less certain. How then—so one is tempted to go on asking—where no Chester Beatty papyrus happens to vouch for the early existence of a Byzantine reading? Are all Byzantine readings ancient? In the cognate case of the Homeric tradition G. Pasquali[11] answers the same question in the affirmative; and, indeed, it seems to me unlikely that the Byzantine editors ever altered the text without manuscript evidence. They left so many hopelessly difficult places unassailed! Their method, I submit, was selection rather than conjecture.[12]

Thus P[46] argues for the Beta texttype as a process, and argues further for an early date for the beginning of that process and for the antiquity of Byzantine readings—though not necessarily for their originality.

One of the Beatty papyri (P[45]), in the Gospel of Mark had the same effect on the Caesarean texttype which had been established by the work of Streeter and of Lake, Blake, and New.[13] The discerning eye of Ayuso saw that P[45] split the Caesarean witnesses into two groups : P[45] fam 1 28 W Orig; and Theta fam 13 565 700.[14] Here also the papyrus witness established a proto-group. Here also it went with "weaker" members against the "leaders" of the type—a fact which Zuntz noted of some of P[46]'s readings within the Alexandrian group. Here also some of the readings of P[45] anticipated Alpha-type readings found in the Textus Receptus.

The Beatty papyrus of the Apocalypse (P[47]) had an equally important influence on the writing of the history of the manuscript tradition of that book. The writing of that history has been the

---

7 (*Chronique d'Egypte*, xxvi, 1951, 200) and Acts xvii. 13. Cf. above, p. 24, n. 3 (Heb. vii. 1). (True also of P[66].)

11 *Storia del tradizione*, 1934, p. 241.

12 *Ibid.*, p. 55.

13 Burnett Hillman Streeter, *The Four Gospels: A Study of Origins* (New York, 1925), chap. IV.

14 T. Ayuso in an article in *Biblica*, 16 (1935), 369-415; this grouping was accepted by the Lakes (in *Studies and Documents*, V [1937], 4, n. 5; and in *Revue Biblique*, XLVIII [1939], 497-505), and this revision of Caesarean grouping is reviewed by B. Metzger in *JBL*, LXIV (1945), 457-89; LXVI (1947), 406-7.

monumental work of Josef Schmid. The results of his life's work are now available in a series of monographs and volumes which are indispensable for any student of this subject.[15] He establishes four texttypes of the Apocalypse. Before his study, previous scholars had made one group of the old uncials A, C, S. Schmid is able with the help of P^{47} to split these into two types : A and C; and P^{47} and S. The other two types are the Andreas type and the *Koine* (Alpha or Byzantine). Schmid demonstrates the superiority of the AC type to all others, the superiority of P^{47}S to the largely "corrected" types, Andreas and K. Here again the early papyrus and its kinfolk seem to me to present a proto-group. The date of the actual documents (P^{47} and Sinaiticus) is earlier than the date of the documents (Alexandrinus and Ephraemi Rescriptus) which contain the best type. I anticipate my criticism of Schmid in saying that P^{47}S can be placed at an early stage in the development of AC.

Just as significant as the discovery of manuscripts is the theoretical work done by scholars. For the reconstruction of the history of the manuscript tradition, the work of the two scholars already quoted is of the greatest value. Josef Schmid in his final volume[16] is explicitly working on this task. This final structure stands on the foundation of his earlier careful studies of groupings of MSS within the major groups; and also—importantly—on his study of the Greek idiom of the Apocalypse. It is not extravagant to say that in comprehensiveness and careful accuracy he has surpassed all previous studies of the Greek manuscript tradition of any part of the New Testament, including the fine work of Ropes on Acts, of the Lakes and their associates on Mark, and of von Soden on the *pericope adulterae*. He has related the existing codices to each other in families, occasionally in tribes, and in texttypes. His work carries our knowledge beyond the stage to which the labors of Hoskier carried it, and it is the library to which the student of any newly discovered manuscript of the Apocalypse must turn for guidance.

Schmid pays Hoskier a deserved tribute for his publication of the manuscript evidence available to him. He also condemns Hoskier, justly, for his fantastic theoretical reconstruction of the tradition. It may be that Schmid was influenced toward caution in this latter

---

[15] *Der Apk-Text des Arethas von Kaisareia und einiger anderer jüngerer gruppen* (Athens, 1936); "Untersuchungen zur Geschichte des griechischen Apk-Textes, Der K-Text" (*Biblica* 17, 1936); *Studien zur Geschichte des griechischen Apokalypse-Textes, 1. Teil: Der Apokalypse-Kommentar des Andreas von Kaisareia, Text* (Munich, 1955); *Einleitung* (Munich, 1956); *2. Teil: Die alten Stämme* (Munich, 1955).

[16] *Studien zur Geschichte des griechischen Apokalypse-Textes, 2. Teil: Die alten Stämme.*

area by Hoskier's failure; at any rate, he leaves the last chapter unwritten.

His summary of results[17] starts off very crisply in numbered paragraphs, which stay brief through number 4.

> In brief, the established results are now put together. In part they consist of clear and certain knowledge; in part they inclose problems for which a definite solution is not possible.
>
> 1. The entire Greek tradition of the Apocalypse-Text divides into four stems, namely AC, P[47]S, Av and K.
> 2. Av and K are two sharply distinct recensions. Their peculiar readings consist for the most part of corrections.
> 3. Av and K are not completely independent of each other (as Bousset and von Soden insisted). They have a common stem which though not extensive is clearly recognizable in a number of common corrections. In several places they contain the original Text against A(C) (P[47])S. It follows from this that they are not merely later forms of the 'older' Text extant in AC and P[47]S.
> 4. The 'older' Text divides again into two Text forms, AC and P[47]S which are to be clearly distinguished. Of these, P[47]S contains a not insignificant number of corrections, while these are almost entirely lacking in the archetype of AC. In one single passage P[47]S alone have the original Text.[18]

But paragraph 5 is as long as the first four together. It begins with the statement that the AC texttype (which includes Oecumenius and the Vulgate) outranks all others in the value of its evidence, but it takes a long paragraph to state that AC is not identical with the Ur-text.

His sixth conclusion is equally lengthy. It argues that since "each of the texttypes has preserved the Ur-text in at least some passages, . . . the texttypes which stand farthest from the original are not to be understood as later, revised forms of their elders in the textual tradition."

In the seventh place, Schmid, recognizing the existence of an interconnection between all texttypes and their constituent parts, concludes "that it is not possible to establish the present connections

[17] *Ibid.*, pp. 146-51.
[18] *Ibid.*, pp. 146-7.

of the major texttypes of the Greek Apocalypse Text-tradition with complete accuracy, and to arrange them all in a *Stemma*." All the texttypes, Schmid concludes, are older than the MSS A and C and reach back at least into the fourth century.

His final (eighth) point reaffirms the relative value of the witnesses in descending order A, C, P[47], S.

Schmid is weak where Zuntz is strong : in the clear recognition of the implication of the data for the interrelationship of the major texttypes. Schmid overrates agreement in the original reading as evidence for common lineage. He underrates the possibility of coincidental agreement in error; e.g. 13 : 7 where in AC, P[47], Av an entire sentence has fallen out as the result of homoioteleuton. The presence of the sentence in S and K shows no more than that the error has not occurred there. As a matter of fact, this omission is not universal in Av (cf. Schmid's edition of the Andreas Commentary [p. 139, apparatus to line 1] which cites three Andreas families and two other Andreas MSS against the omission), nor is it universal in K.

But the major mistake is made in thinking of the "old texttypes" as frozen blocks, even after admitting that no one manuscript is a perfect witness to any texttype. *If* no one MS is a perfect witness to any type, then all witnesses are mixed in ancestry (or individually corrupted, and thus parents of mixture). The mixture was, we are certain, partial.[19] It did not remove all original readings; it did not remove all the distinctive readings of the texttype to which the codex belonged. Beyond this we now recognize that the texttypes developed, they grew, they are a process starting in the second century and proceeding by selection from available readings, from available "good, old MSS," and proceeding also into new paths under local standards of excellence in syntax and in doctrine.

Quae cum ita sint, agreements of the late texttype K with an early texttype or MS in the original reading is due to the survival of that original reading in some one of the various channels that make up the complex ancestry of K. Agreements of this kind do *not* move K as an entity (as a texttype) back to the date of the earlier texttype or MS. Even if, and it is too big an if, every reading found in K existed somewhere in the second century, K did not exist in the second century. If the term "texttype" means anything, it means that entire complex of readings in its total pattern which we refer to as "the Alpha texttype" or "the Byzantine text" or "the K text-

---

[19] *Ibid.;* Schmid gives evidence for this again and again in the course of his work.

type." This did not exist as the dominant element in any MS in the second century. It does exist in the ninth century and later. The clinching evidence for the date of a texttype is a datable MS *belonging* to it, or a Church Father who uses it as Cyprian used the "Western" type found in K.

Schmid's first five conclusions are solidly established, and the ranking of the four oldest witnesses in his eighth seems equally sound. But the claim in number 6 that the later texttypes are not revised forms of their elders seems doubtful. All that has been proved is that they are not *entirely* derived from their elders. If, however, there stands "at the beginning of the text a text handled by humble piety and therefore a text with little unity," all texttypes must derive from this and/or from each other plus a modicum of "new" editorial contribution. What needs clarification in Schmid's sixth conclusion is not only the meaning of "later" *in re* a texttype, but also the meaning of a "revised form" of an older texttype. Revision almost universally proceeded on a documentary basis. MSS from outside the texttype were used to revise it. This opened a door through which Ur-text readings could be added just as surely as it opened the door to alien corrections and corruptions.[20] This challenges also his seventh conclusion that a stemma of texttypes cannot be made. I am confident that he has supplied the data that makes this possible—at least in large outlines.

To focus the material surveyed here into sharp statement as a basis for criticism and further study is the purpose of the following propositions :

  1. *A texttype is a process, not the work of one hand.*

Scholars have been forced to the conclusion that a texttype is a process not from the study of the loosely-connected "Western" witnesses but from the study of the Beta texttype—Hort's "neutral." This was implicit in Hort's own identification of his "Alexandrian" text, intimately related to his Neutral. Vaganay's argument for process came from his study of the relationship of P^{45} to the Beta texttype in Luke and John. Zuntz's argument has been quoted above (pp. 131-32). Schmid sharply differentiates Av and K from AC and P^{47}S, and the differentiation includes the recognition of process as more extensive in AC and P^{47}S than in the other two

---

[20] But before Schmid's argument for a fourth-century date for Av is rejected, the evidence (which Schmid refers to) of S^a's (the fourth century corrector of Sinaiticus) agreement with Av must be explained—Schmid, *op. cit.*, p. 129. Schmid's argument here rests on his acceptance of the conclusions drawn by Bousset (*Studien*, pp. 42-44). Bousset's work should be reviewed in the light of current understanding of the history of texttypes.

types. My own earlier study of the Beta texttype in Mark drove me to the recognition of "process" in the formation of a texttype.[21]

2. *The Vulgate Versions were the work of one hand and were editions as well as translations.*

3. *The Greek Vulgate—The Byzantine or Alpha texttype—had in its origin no such single focus as the Latin had in Jerome. Like Jerome's Vulgate it had several revised editions.*

4. *Origen did not make an edition (create a texttype) of the Greek New Testament.*

5. *The so-called Western text or Delta texttype is the uncontrolled popular text of the second century. It has no unity and should not be referred to as the "Western text."*

(*a*) Even Zuntz (with whom I find it hard to differ) once refers to the text of the New Testament in the second century as if it were a unity : "The final result was the survival of a text far superior to that of the second century . . ." (quoted above, p. 131). Schmid did not work out the inter-relations of his four types except that he grouped the first two (AC and $P^{47}S$) as closer to each other than they were to the last two, and the last two (Av and K) as closer to each other than they were to the first two. (*b*) Schmid's work is limited to the Greek tradition, which does not contain the equivalent of MS D. Without D and the versions in the Gospel of John, where would we find this texttype(s)? (*c*) If the answer is "the Fathers," Schmid's findings still seem to exclude "Western" types. Origen's text is generally identical with $P^{47}S$, Hippolytus of Rome with AC Oec. Irenaeus seems not very different from AC Oec; and Clement, Alexandrinus, Eusebius, Methodius have few, inconclusive quotes (pp. 156-171). (*d*) Did the Apocalypse enjoy widespread popular usage in the second century?

Is it far-fetched to regard his type $P^{47}S$ as a stage on the way from the second-century types to the "better" Beta texttype of AC Oec? As such a stage $P^{47}S$ Orig would contain a number of readings which earlier nomenclature would have labelled as "Western," meaning early non-Neutral. Schmid, by his separation of $P^{47}S$ Orig from the "Neutral" AC Oec, is saying the same thing. He will not call them "Western" in a geographical sense because of the absence of Latin support. But Western has ceased to be a geographical term for a long time.

6. *The Beta texttype (Hort's "Neutral") is a "made" text probably Alexandrian in origin, produced in part by the selection of relatively "good old MSS" but more importantly by the philological editorial know-how of Alexandrians.* Zuntz's reconstruction of this process is superb.

[21] *See* "Genealogical Method," *JBL*, LXI (1947), pp. 119, 123.

7. *The so-called Caesarean texttype is not Caesarean and is at least two types, the earlier of which is a proto-type, an early stage in the process which produced the mature Beta and Delta texttypes.*

8. *It follows from number* 1, *as also from the textual data, that the earliest witness to a texttype is never the archetype of the texttype.*

Thus Schmid tells us that P is not the archetype of Av, and Q even less the archetype of K. He shows that P⁴⁷ and S, though earlier than A and C, are not as good witnesses as the later MSS. The Lakes identified Theta 700 and 565 as the strongest Caesarean witnesses in Mark, but P⁴⁵ is the earliest and agrees with the weaker witnesses. A in the Gospels is the earliest member of the Alpha texttype, but it does not fit into any of the major editions of that type, not even Family π, as Silva Lake has shown. P⁶⁶ can be claimed for the Beta texttype in John but it is far from the center of the group. Zuntz put P⁴⁶ with 1739 and B as, at times, a proto-Beta texttype in the Epistles. His inclusion of B is in my judgment an error. *Some* of the readings of B are derived from the proto-Beta texttype of which P⁴⁶ is a member, but we cannot relocate an entire MS on the basis of a small minority of its readings.

9. *The textual history of the New Testament differs from corpus to corpus, and even from book to book; therefore the witnesses have to be regrouped in each new section.*

Schmid shows this in striking fashion for the Apocalypse vis-à-vis the Praxapostolos:

> Bei der über 80 HSS umfassenden K-gruppe lässt sich feststellen, das Schwester-HSS im Apk-Text dies fast niemals auch im Praxapostolos sind, und dass umgekehrt Schwester-HSS im Praxapostolos fast nie in der Apk unmittelbare Schwestern sind.

He then gives more than half-a-dozen examples.²²

10. *As in dating documents, so in dating texttypes what is needed is a datable witness to the type, not only to some of its readings, for the overwhelming majority of readings were created before the year 200. But very few, if any, texttypes were established by that time.*

The agreement of Origen with P⁴⁷ in the Apocalypse and with P⁴⁵ in Mark exhorts us to pay more attention to date in interpreting the history of the tradition in the future. Thus in writing the history of the texttypes we should begin with the earliest witness, as Zuntz did in his study of the Epistles.

---

²² Schmid, *op. cit.*, pp. 37-38. See my examples of alternations of type even within one manuscript in "Grouping of New Testament Manuscripts," *NTS*, IV (1958), pp. 89-90.

XIV | *Allen Wikgren*
| UNIVERSITY OF CHICAGO

HISTORY AND
SCRIPTURE

Christianity has been called the religion of a book, and there is a high degree of truth in the statement, especially with reference to its Protestant forms. The earliest Christians as Jews inherited among other things a body of Scripture which they naturally adopted and used as their own. In spite of voices to the contrary—such as in Marcionism—they retained this heritage even as Gentiles, recognizing and affirming as they did their religious continuity with the past. But the new, spirit-guided movement could not be contained in old wineskins; a newly centered and motivated faith called for new expression. This in turn, however, gave rise to written documents, which as time passed became the sacred books of the new Way. How these, joined to the old, became Christian Scripture and normative for the faith is a wellknown story.

But the resulting situation, especially in view of developments in post-Reformation Protestantism, raised serious problems about the nature and function of this Bible. A Christian Scripture which included the "Old Testament" continued to be a vexing item, with some revival of Marcionite tendencies on the one hand to depreciate or eliminate the "Old," e.g., by Harnack and Schleiermacher, and with various attempts more recently on the other hand to define a "unity" of the Bible.[1] Serious questions also have continued to be

---

[1] Cf., e.g., C. H. Dodd, *The Authority of the Bible* (London, 1928); A. M. Hunter, *The Unity of the New Testament* (London, 1943); R. E. Davies, *The Problem of Authority in the Continental Reformers* (London, 1926); A. G. Hebert, *The Authority of the Old Testament* (London, 1947); J. W. C. Wand, *The Authority of the Scriptures* (London, 1949); Gunnar Ostborn, *Cult and Canon* (Uppsala, 1950); R. R. Williams, *Authority in the Apostolic Age* (London, 1950); H. H. Rowley, *The Unity of the Bible* (London, 1953); A. Richardson and W. Schweizer, eds., *Biblical Authority for Today* (London, 1951); J. K. S. Reid, *The Authority of*

139

raised concerning the authority of Scripture in relation to that of the community of faith out of which it comes and within which it functions, as well as in a wider significance as the "Word of God." Recent interest in "biblical theology" has led to a reexamination of these and other aspects of the total problem from the standpoint both of biblical scholarship and of theology.[2] But because of diversities of presuppositions and method, in addition to the intrinsic difficulties, proposed solutions cannot be regarded as satisfactory to one and all. They have become involved, also, in the revival of interest in Reformation theology, the "demythologizing" controversy, "existentialism," and the problem of the meaning of history and related matters.

In the interests of progress through some mutual contribution from what may be differentiated as a "biblical-historical" and a "biblical-theological" orientation, it may not be amiss to raise a question regarding basic assumptions which seem to divide participants in the discussion. In particular we have in mind here the paradoxical character which appears to attach to the treatment of history on the part of at least a large segment of the theologically-oriented movement. A virtual disregard of history and of historical methodology on the one hand seems to be combined on the other with an appeal to history in the definition of the nature and authority of the Bible. Christianity is emphasized to be a historical religion, and the assertion that God has revealed himself in the events of history has become a cliché in this appeal. How seriously, we may ask, is this to be taken in terms of what we mean by history? Is it simply a theological abstraction or "theologoumenon"?

There is little doubt that in connection with the problem of Bible the conception of "history" here encountered generally means a particular strand of the story of mankind, namely, the Judeo-Christian. A divine plan of salvation is found to be mediated through the historical and cultural process in a theonomous, covenanted community of faith. This sacred history or "Heilsgeschichte" gives its distinctive character to the Judeo-Christian faith and tradition. Characteristic of this emphasis is an appeal to certain events in history in which men encountered God, the climax and center of which for the Christian is his redemptive work in that cluster or structure of happenings which may be called the event of Jesus Christ. Faith becomes a commitment to God as thus known and

---

the Scriptures (London, 1957); R. Abba, *The Nature and Authority of the Bible* (London, 1958); and E. Kraeling, *The Old Testament since the Reformation* (London, 1955).

[2] *See* note 1.

involves a way of life commensurate with the divine nature and will as revealed in Christ and summed up in terms of *agape*. This *agape* is expressed in and through a fellowship engaged in proclaiming the good news of the Reign of God and of bringing its claim to all men. Implicit throughout is an emphasis on the reality of time, i.e., upon history as having direction and movement, a consistent purpose and goal. It is a particularistic and teleological interpretation, but as a reconstruction of Christian theology we need not for our present purposes question its main propositions, especially if these are worked out in connection with history as a whole.[3]

A real difficulty arises, however, when we are asked to narrow the scope of what is meant by "history" by limiting our documentation of these crucial "events" to the canonical Scriptures. This delimitation will often mean not only the use of a modern, Protestant Bible with the books arranged in a traditional, Protestant order, but also a restricted employment even of this resource, through an eclectic process dictated by the cultural and theological preconditioning of the interpreter. Yet studies in the history of the biblical canon have confirmed what we learn from history itself, namely, that the essential norm or canon was in the faith of the believing community, of which the documents constituted but the literary expression. True, this particular collection may be considered of unique significance as containing the first-hand and classical expression of the faith in its initial, creative and greatest period; but in respect to the total possible documentation—literary or otherwise—of the history and culture of the period involved, it is a partial and to some extent a fortuitous representation. For this reason the biblical scholar, whatever his canonical Scriptures on Sunday—or Saturday—will avail himself of all possible sources of information in his reconstruction and understanding of the life and faith of the period from "Genesis to Revelation." From this viewpoint only a limited basis of discourse may result from a theological orientation which understands "biblical" to mean simply "canonical."

A simple test which may be applied in order to evaluate the relationship between profession and practice would be the use made of the "intertestamental" literature. We think here primarily of the so-called Old Testament Apocrypha since they have been part of the canon—and still are, in large segments of "Christendom"—

---

[3] Cf. H. Butterfield, *Christianity and History* (London, 1949); R. Niebuhr, *Faith and History* (London, 1949); R. Shinn, *Christianity and the Problem of History* (New York, 1953); J. Daniélou, *The Lord of History: reflections on the inner meaning of history* (transl. by N. Abercrombie; London and Chicago, 1958); see also note 17, p. 145

although the other literature of the period is no less valuable for the light it sheds upon the canonical documents and the historical matrix of the Judeo-Christian religious movement. [4]

For the biblical scholar or the historian of religion it is unnecessary to emphasize the crucial significance of this epoch for an understanding of Christian origins. One may even say that without its religious developments a Christian movement as we know it would have been unlikely. It is enough to mention the area of apocalypticism, with its elaboration of thought regarding the messiah, resurrection and judgment and final destinies for the individual, angelology, demonology, etc. We are fortunate in having a great deal of literary evidence for all this, significantly increased now by the Qumran documents. But the latter have also served to remind us that a definite historical-cultural situation is always involved, and it is here that one must seek that basic continuity of religious thought and structure which alone can validate any so-called "unity" which may be seen in the canonical Scriptures or any ultimate authority which they may have or may mediate. [5] Yet contemporary treatments of the unity and authority of the Bible— and even its theology—are with few exceptions far from satisfactory in this matter.

Our concern here is not primarily with works which are consciously limited in scope by dogmatic or other presuppositions, although such works generally exhibit no little concern about establishing a continuity not only between the historical Jesus and the apostolic witness, but also between these and the credal formulas of the subsequent centuries; [6] and it is difficult then to see by what logic the developments of the immediate foreground of nascent Christianity should be excluded. Actually, they are not so excluded in truly historical reconstructions, for even a "fundamentalist"

---

[4] H. H. Farmer, in his treatment, "The Bible, Its Significance and Authority," *The Interpreter's Bible*, I (Nashville, 1952), 3-31, indicates that the status of the Apocrypha is an open question; but his suggestion that they "are available" is not of much help in answering the question. J. K. S. Reid, in his volume on the authority of the Bible (*op. cit.*), ranges learnedly over much territory, and often sees (and to some extent avoids) various pitfalls in the theological "solutions" proposed. But the end result contributes little to the solution of the main problem, and the approach is purely canonical, with no effective attention to the literature and history of the intertestamental period.

[5] E.g., in *The Ancient Library of Qumran* (London, 1958) Frank Cross observes that "the eschatological existence of the church will no longer appear as a unique phenomenon but as the continuation of the communal and apocalyptic tradition developed at Qumran" (p. 148).

[6] E.g., in the recent summary of Vincent Taylor, *The Person of Christ in New Testament Teaching* (London and New York, 1958).

may wax rhetorical about the "fullness of time" while at the same time skipping nonchalantly from Malachi (see below) to Matthew in discussing the unity of the Bible.

Our concern also is not primarily with such Old Testament studies as may argue or presume that they are treating a definite body of literature and history. These, if they are sound, must take account of their own appropriate background and *Sitz-im-Leben*. However, when they deal with such comprehensive themes as "Old Testament Theology" and come to treat such special topics as the resurrection and the future life, they will be hard pressed to avoid reference to the literature and thought of the "intertestamental" period. Yet some of them are able to do so! And when this orientation is basically that of a "biblical theology" or *A Christian Theology of the Old Testament*, as a recent title has it,[7] there is even less justification for such a self-imposed limitation. Yet it is characteristic of many if not most of the recent treatments of "Old Testament Theology" of this kind.

We are involved here with an aspect of the difficult problem of method in the treatment of the "theology of the Old Testament," but one which usually has been inadequately dealt with in the several discussions which have been called forth by the recent revival of interest in the total subject.[8] Professor Dentan, although he has himself written an appreciative account of the Apocrypha, simply states in his monograph on method that the scope of Old Testament theology "should properly be limited to the canonical

---

[7] George F. Knight (London, 1959). He mentions the Dead Sea Scrolls, but little else.

[8] Cf. Robert C. Dentan, *Preface to Old Testament Theology* (New Haven, 1950), in his discussion and bibliography; Ivan Engnell in his paper at the Oxford Congress of Old Testament scholars, 1959, "Methodological Aspects of Old Testament Study," published in *Vetus Testamentum*, Suppl. Vol. VII (Leiden, 1960). Professor Engnell, while not directly concerned with the subject, recognizes the "very delicate problem of how to work out the 'distinctive character' of O.T. literature and religion as well as the possibility or writing, in a scientific manner, a 'theology of the O.T.' " But however it be done, "it must nevertheless be accomplished in a purely historical way" (p. 30). For a contrary viewpoint see James D. Smart, "The Death and Rebirth of Old Testament Theology," *JR* XXIII (1943), 1-11, 125-136; and for an incisive criticism of the standpoint there expressed cf. W. A. Irwin, "The Reviving Theology of the Old Testament," *JR*, XXV (1945), 235-246. Cf. also the recent discussions in German by Franz Hesse, "Kerygma oder geschichtliche Wirklichkeit," *Zeitschrift für Theologie und Kirche* 57 (1960), 17-26; and Rolf Rendtorff, "Hermeneutik des Alten Testaments als Frage der Geschichte," *Ibid.*, pp. 27-40. Further bibliography on the total subject will also be found here. Cf. also note 9.

books." [9] He would refer all the other literature to "Introduction to New Testament Theology" and to "History of the New Testament Period." This is a generous gesture, and one can well sympathize with it in view of the enormous amount of data with which the Old Testament scholar must be concerned. Critical New Testament scholarship naturally has not neglected these documents, but at the same time it profits much from the judgments of those who would come to them with a more specialized knowledge of their religious backgrounds and—in the case of most of them—of the languages in which they were originally written. [10] Happily, they have received increased attention now for several decades by Old Testament scholarship, [11] even, as we have noted, in some of the new treatments of Old Testament theology. [12] Professor Burrows, in fact, frankly states that "Some of them are actually as valuable and truly inspired as some of the books that were retained [in the canon], or more so." [13]

But our concern is not primarily with the question of whether this literature should be regarded as canonical or not. It is rather

[9] p. 55. He notes here that early critical treatments for the most part included the intertestamental literature but that the later works (i.e., in the theological revival period) did not. Exceptions indicated are Edward König and E. Sellin. To these should be added Millar Burrows and perhaps Gerhard von Rad. However, König (1912, 2nd ed., 1915) really belongs to an intermediate period, and Sellin, in spite of being ostensibly more "historical" than "dogmatic" is dogmatically oriented in his approach and makes minor use of the non-canonical writings. We might, of course, add here such treatments as those of A. Loisy (1933), W. Boussett (1926), and Oesterley and Robinson (2nd ed., 1937), but these probably would be denominated as "religions-geschichtlich" in their emphasis rather than "theological" (as we perforce are using the term in this discussion). The recent survey, *The Religion of the Bible* (New York, 1960), by S. Vernon McCasland, includes the Apocrypha.

[10] Exclusion of Jewish scholarship from consideration here is simply by virtue of a limitation of our attention to Christian syntheses. Jewish scholars have contributed much to the elucidation of New Testament backgrounds, particularly from the rabbinic writings, and currently they are widely engaged in studies in the intertestamental literature; witness the series, *Jewish Apocryphal Literature*. Jewish interpreters, to be sure, have had their own problem in the past regarding the use of some of these writings, in particular Ecclesiasticus. *See*, e.g., Cecil Roth, "Ecclesiasticus in the Synagogue Service," *JBL*, LXXI (1952), 171-78, for an interesting documentation of the use of the book and its familiarity to the Jews down to the 10th/11th centuries. The important Jewish treatments and texts are noted.

[11] See the surveys by J. Coert Rylaarsdam ("Intertestamental Studies Since Charles's Apocrypha and Pseudepigrapha") and by Ralph Marcus ("The Future of Intertestamental Studies") in *The Study of the Bible Today and Tomorrow*, ed. by H. R. Willoughby (Chicago, 1947).

[12] *See* Note 9.   [13] *Op. cit.*, p. 19.

with the methodology which gives lip service to historical method and historical continuity while denying them in the name of "theology" by an eclectic use of sources. However, since these contemporary "syntheses" are undoubtedly—and admittedly—executed in the interest of a (Protestant) "unity" of the Bible or a "Christian" Old Testament by such method, it may not be amiss to propose realistically with Professor John Cheek that the Apocrypha be included in what he calls the "permissive canon," that is the total collection from which a functional canon emerges consisting of those parts found useful in the support of certain "biblical" doctrines.[14]

Yet—and paradoxically it seems—exponents of a Christian (or "biblical") philosophy of history assume that a selected group of events gives meaning to *all* history. What is left, writes Karl Lowith, are "spurious happenings" unless they are judged significant "in the perspective of their possible signification of judgment and salvation."[15] This is frankly theology, of course, not history. There are no "spurious happenings" for the historian. And who is to make this evaluation is not indicated! Similarly, Raymond Abba suggests that the unity of the Bible is "not a literary unity, neither is it an historical unity; it is a theological unity."[16] To his credit, however, it may be said that he recognizes the Apocrypha as a "valuable link" between the Old Testament and the New, and while regarding them on a "lower spiritual level" to Christians in general, he finds (with C. H. Dodd) a "notable exception" in the events of the Maccabean revolt. The theological emphasis is found also in such diversely oriented writings as those of Nicolas Berdyaev, Paul Tillich and H. Butterfield.[17] It is a general characteristic of such expositions that where attempts are made to state a "Christian philosophy of history," this is framed in propositions of such a

[14] "The Apocrypha in Christian Scripture," *JBR*, XXVI (1958), 207-12. Cf. a Roman Catholic viewpoint by L.-M. Dewailly in "Canon du Nouveau Testament et histoire des dogmes," *Vivre et Penser* 50 (1941), p. 92: "S'il s'agit de distinguer une canonicité passive, celle des livres proclamés canonique, et une canonicité active, celle de leur caractère régulateur." This was the kind of distinction applied to the Apocrypha by Jerome, in which he is followed by the Anglican Church in the use of these documents.

[15] *Meaning in History* (Chicago, 1949), p. 185.

[16] *Op. cit.*, p. 3.

[17] Nicolas Berdyaev, *The Meaning of History* (Eng. tr., London, 1936) and other writings; Paul Tillich, *The Interpretation of History* (Eng. tr., London and New York, 1936); H. Butterfield, *op. cit.* ("The Christian interpretation of history is a thing which we bring to our history and super-impose upon it. . . ." —p. 23). Cf. Professor Danielou's observation that "Professional historians tend to take all these large generalizations with a grain of salt" (*op. cit.*, p. 96).

general and sweeping character that they are on the one hand eclectic so far as the canonical Scriptures are concerned and on the other cannot possibly be confined to these as distinct from similar writings of the same period. This type of interpretation, however, does not usually claim to be "biblical," although the tendency is often present to equate "Christian" with "biblical" in terms of our canon.

The first Christians themselves, as we have already indicated, were well aware that their faith was inseparably connected with that of their spiritual forebears. While their efforts to demonstrate and document this continuity also tended to become channeled and restricted by inherited canonical limitations and to be characterized by an often dubious methodology, they were at all events bearing witness in their own way to a fundamental truth. But that there was also a certain freedom present is attested both by the use of extra-canonical writings[18] and by protests against attempts to stifle the "living and abiding voice" through reducing it to written media. Faith itself was the unifying principle which bound them together to themselves as well as to their fellow-believers of the past.[19] At the same time it was necessary in combatting Gnosticism to emphasize the historical nexus of the faith and the interconnection of its successive stages, a concern reflected in several of the early Church Fathers and worked out especially by Gregory of Nyssa, using the term ἀκολουθία, which was employed by Aristotle in regard to laws governing physical motion and change.[20]

For the early Christian church, also, the historical gap between Old and New Testaments was not so serious as is assumed by the common Protestant view that the Old Testament consists of the books from Genesis to Malachi.[21] Actually there is no tangible

[18] The argument *e silentio* that the New Testament writers do not cite the Apocrypha is of little significance here. Several Old Testament books are not cited either. The situation is similar to that of the Apostolic Fathers in relation to the New Testament books. Acquaintance and usage are clear in regard to a number of the Apocrypha and Pseudepigrapha, and the fact of such usage in Palestine is now attested by the Qumran community. Cf. A.C. Sundberg ,Jr., "The Old Testament of the Early Church," *Harvard Theological Review*, LI (1958), 205-26.

[19] Cf. S. Vernon McCasland, "The Unity of the Scriptures," *JBL*, LXXIII (1954), 1-10.

[20] Cf. Jean Danielou, *op. cit.*, chap. 6, "The Development of History."

[21] There is in fact no certainty that the Old Testament canon as we know it was so defined until toward the end of the first century A.D. The third division of the Jewish canon, "The Writings," was still open, and the "closing" of the canon no doubt in part constituted an attempt to exclude writings of heretical and Christian groups.

evidence earlier than the fourth century A.D. that the Old Testament ended in that way, and this is in a Christian list. In terms of religious value and chronological sequence the Hebrew canon—if it were ever contained in one scroll or codex—would have ended with the Hagiographa, probably, as in the Masoretic text, with Esther, Daniel, Ezra-Nehemiah, Chronicles. A similar order may be assumed for primitive Jewish-Christian usage, and it is to some extent reflected in the earliest lists and manuscripts. However, the evidence is no earlier than the second century, and most of it is from the fourth and fifth. By this time the matter is complicated by the inclusion of the Apocrypha as part of the Old Testament in Greek, the Septuagint. In a total of some twenty-seven items of Christian evidence available in the earliest period, the Old Testament ends in twelve different ways as follows: Daniel—7; II Maccabee—6; Malachi—3 (i.e., the Twelve Minor Prophets); Psalms—2; Esther—2; Wisdom of Sirach—2; Ezekiel—1; Song of Songs—1; II Esdras—1; Tobit—1; Rest of Baruch—1. The position of Daniel is owing to the fact that when the prophetic canon stood last, the Twelve generally preceded the combination Isaiah, Jeremiah, Ezekiel, Daniel. Thus the ending with Daniel or II Maccabees accounts for nearly half of the lists or manuscripts and brings the chronological period down to *ca.* 165 B.C. The inclusion of II Esdras (generally associated with Ezra-Nehemiah) may be said, however, to close the gap completely;[22] in fact, its introductory and concluding chapters (1, 2, 13, 14) are generally regarded as Christian interpolations. But in the Septuagint—followed by the Latin Vulgate—the Old Testament came to end generally with II Maccabees.

The unsatisfactory historical data furnished for an important segment of the period by the vague symbolism of the apocalyptic writings such as Daniel and II Esdras led also to the use of Josephus' accounts to fill in the chronological lacunae. Josephus' works were thus preserved by Christian usage. They are cited verbatim by Eusebius. The *Antiquities* and *Jewish War* are even to be found in an extant Latin manuscript Bible of the thirteenth century, the codex Gigas in Stockholm, although the resultant size of the manuscript is such that two men are required to lift it. Evidence of such usage in close connection with the Bible continues in the age of printing. A Latin Bible first published in 1553 by John Oporinus at Basel contains selections from Josephus arranged specifically for the

---

[22] After the Council of Trent, II Esdras and the Prayer of Manasses were given as an appendix to the Bible.

purpose of filling in the period from Esdras to Maccabees and from Maccabees to the advent of Christ.[23] The main point here again is not the question of the canon, but the demonstration of Christian appreciation of the historical and religious developments of the "intertestamental" period in the use and understanding of the canonical literature. It would seem then to be an eminently fair test of the seriousness with which the term "history" is used in theological interpretations of the nature, authority and message of the Bible to inquire about the validity which these see in the evidence of the "intertestamental" period for their reconstructions and "solutions."

While serious questions may thus be raised concerning the methodology in terms of its own presuppositions, even more serious ones have been propounded in terms of *Religionsgeschichte, Weltgeschichte*, and of modern thought in general on the grounds that it may represent too narrow and mythical a view of history in its ideational syntheses.[24] To deal with this criticism is beyond the scope of the present discussion; but we may say that such a characterization need not be true and that it was not really true of most of the biblical writers themselves, for they give ample evidence of attempting to see the activity of God in terms of universal history.[25] The accounts of beginnings in Genesis sought to explain the origins of the world and of all nations. The prophetic achievement of monotheism carried the implication of universalism. The insights of the sages were largely directed to problems and situations common

[23] Its title page includes the statement: " . . . & adiecit ex Flavio Iosepho historiae supplementum ab Esdrae temporibus usque ad Machabaeos, itemque a Machabaeis usque ad Christum." The "Latin History Bibles" of the manuscript period made much use of Josephus; and the widely known one of Peter Comestor (Historia Scholastica) was issued in some thirteen printed editions between 1473 and 1500.

[24] *Cf.* A. Wilder, "Biblical Authority for Today," *JBL* XXXI (1952), 183ff., who observes, among other things, that the metaphysical implications of the "word of God" theology are not clear; J. Wach, "General Revelation and the Religions of the World," *JBR*, XXII (1954), 83-93; B. Meland, "Some Unresolved Issues of Theology," *JR*, XXIV (1944), 233-39; A. W. Munk, *History and God* (New York, 1952), *passim;* R. Niebuhr, *op. cit.*, p. 58 ("Man's growing reason insists on greater and greater consistency in relating realms of supernal mystery to each other and to the structures of coherence which are empirically observed in nature and in history.") and p. 121 ("It would seem therefore that the story of mankind is progressively becoming one story, both through an actual growth in cultural interpenetration and through the development of historical sciences, able to trace and analyze such interpenetrations").

[25] Treatments of a "Christian philosophy of history" generally agree that it demands a universalistic orientation. Cf. R. G. Collingwood, *The Philosophy of History* (London, 1930), p. 49

to all mankind. The apocalyptic movement, whatever its failings, was concerned with the future and ultimate destinies of *all* men. The *praeparatio evangelica* was Gentile as well as Jewish. The gospel of the Kingdom in Jesus' teaching about divine providence and in the apostolic proclamations was universal in scope. Insofar, also, as "biblical theology" may speak of a faith which involved the release of a new spirit and power in the world and which gives direction and meaning to history as a whole, it would appear to have a universalistic and contemporary relevance and significance. If, however, it is made to consist of theological abstractions imposed upon the historical process and involving a divorce of faith from history, its validity will naturally come under question.

But the matter of congeniality with modern thought is not to be taken as a denial or minimization of such discontinuities of special or unique significance as have appeared in the Judeo-Christian and Christian history and tradition. These, however, really can only be identified and appreciated against their appropriate historical and religious contexts. Likewise, as aspects of these, the unity and authority of the Bible are functions of the historical manifestations of the faith, and an understanding of their meaning will be inadequate when limited to a literary-canonical orientation. An adequate synthesis will be one which takes account of the total period and which thus takes seriously its own theoretical propositions regarding the disclosure of God in history, recognizing at the same time that "the Word of God is not bound," and that it is not ultimately a matter of words and syllables, however significant and indispensable certain of these are to the community of faith. Such comprehensiveness of treatment will not only contribute to a fuller understanding and appreciation of Christian origins and thought, but will also serve to make increasingly possible that wider synthesis of religious concern—involving biblical scholar, theologian, and philosopher and historian of religion—which has become of vital significance in the contemporary world, rampant as it is with the destructive forces of militarism and secularism.

HAROLD RIDEOUT WILLOUGHBY

Harold Rideout Willoughby was born in North Haverhill, New Hampshire, on March 3, 1890. After receiving the A.B. degree (1915) and an M.A. degree in Classics (1916) at Wesleyan University, he took a B.D. degree in 1918 from Garrett Biblical Institute. He also held the positions of Squire Teaching Fellow in Greek at Wesleyan University (1915-16) and Gustavus F. Swift Fellow at American University (1919-20). He then came as a student to the University of Chicago, where he pursued work in the Divinity School with specialization in New Testament studies. Following an interruption by World War I, in which he served as a chaplain and a sergeant in the field artillery, he completed his academic course and received the Ph.D. degree *summa cum laude* in 1924. In the same year he was appointed to the faculty of the Divinity School and the Department of New Testament and Early Christian Literature at the University of Chicago. After an eventful and distinguished career of over thirty years he reached retirement age and on July 1, 1955, became Professor Emeritus of Early Christian Origins.

Special honors which have come to him include election to Phi Beta Kappa, eight special lectureships, two honorary degrees (D.D., Litt.D.), and membership in a dozen learned societies. Of these and other activities one may read in *Who's Who in America*, *World Biography*, and similar sources. The scholarly and wide-ranging aspects of his special interests are evident in the bibliography of his writings which accompanies this sketch. Among these special concerns one may mention particularly his notable contributions in areas of early Christian origins and backgrounds, exemplified by his widely known *Pagan Regeneration*, and in New Testament and Byzantine art and iconography, exemplified by such studies as that of the Rockefeller-McCormick New Testament, and in Early Christian archeology and English Bible. During his presidency of the Chicago Society of Biblical Research in 1945-46 he conceived and carried to subsequent publication the monumental symposium, *The Study of the Bible Today and Tomorrow*. As may be seen also from the Bibliography, Professor Willoughby became literary executor for President Ernest DeWitt Burton of the University of Chicago, after the latter's death in 1925.

As a student and colleague of President Burton and other of his contemporaries, Professor Willoughby became a vital link with the original eye-witnesses of the moving events of the University's beginnings. Moreover, he has throughout his career continued to be an exponent of those ideals which made the University great. In his later faculty years also, in spite of his well-known aversion to administrative duties, he has yielded to calls upon his wisdom and experience and unselfish devotion to the best interests of the University to serve in various administrative capacities in areas of University life. These have included membership on the Council and the Committee of the Council of the University Senate and on the Policy Committee of the Division of the Humanities, of which committee he was the "spokesman" at the time of his retirement.

Alumni of the University know Professor Willoughby as a friend who has continued a close and helpful interest in their careers. Much of this stems from his association with students as head of Goodspeed Hall when it was the residence hall for Divinity School men, a position which he held from 1919 to 1936. He maintained a prolific correspondence with the alumni and for many years was the chief source of such news items about them as appeared in "The Divinity School News."

It is a matter of great satisfaction to report that his continuing influence even in "retirement" mitigates to some extent the distinct loss to the University of that singular combination of qualities of true religious conviction and concern, unwavering devotion to truth, exacting scholarship, and University statesmanship such as he has exemplified.

SPECIAL LECTURESHIPS HELD BY HAROLD R. WILLOUGHBY

Garrett Biblical Institute (Bennet Lecture in Early Christian Archeology), 1938, 1939.

American Schools of Oriental Research, Jerusalem, 1937.

Nashotah House, Wisconsin, 1937.

Chicago Presbyterian Theological Seminary, 1933.

McCormick Theological Seminary, 1938.

Oberlin Graduate School of Theology (Haskell Lectures), 1948.

Queens University, Canada (Theological Alumni Association Lecture), 1952.

Iliff School of Theology (Visiting Professor), 1957.

BIBLIOGRAPHY OF HAROLD R. WILLOUGHBY

BOOKS

1. *Pagan Regeneration: A Study of Mystery Initiations in the Graeco-Roman World*. Chicago : University of Chicago Press, 1939. Pp. xi + 307.

2. *The Rockefeller McCormick New Testament*, Vol. III, *The Miniatures*. Chicago : University of Chicago Press, 1932. Pp. xliv + 368 + cxxv plates.

3. *Codex 2400 and its Miniatures*. New York : College Art Association, 1933. Pp. 74 + 74 figs. + 11 plates.

4. *The Coverdale Psalter and the Quatrocentenary of the Printed English Bible*. Chicago : The Caxton Club, 1935. Pp. 95.

5. *The Four Gospels of Karahissar*, Vol. II, *The Cycle of Text Illustrations*. Chicago : University of Chicago Press, 1936. Pp. xxxvi + 496 + cxxxvii plates.

6. *The Elizabeth Day McCormick Apocalypse*, Vol. I, *A Greek Corpus of Revelation Iconography*. Chicago : University of Chicago Press, 1940. Pp. xxxii + 602 + lxxii plates (Fiftieth Anniversary Publication of the University of Chicago Press).

7. *The First Authorized English Bible and the Cranmer Preface*. Chicago : University of Chicago Press, 1942. Pp. x + 50 + 7 plates.

8. *The Rockefeller McCormick Manuscript and What Came of It: A Bibliographical Record*. Chicago : New Testament Department, 1943. Pp. iv + 12 + 2 plates.

9. *Soldiers' Bibles Through Three Centuries*. Chicago : University of Chicago Press, 1944. Pp. viii + 44 + 16.

BOOKS EDITED

1. *A Short Introduction to the Gospels*. With Ernest DeWitt Burton. Chicago : University of Chicago Press, 1926. Pp. x + 159.

2. *Christianity in the Modern World: Papers and Addresses of Ernest DeWitt Burton*. Chicago : University of Chicago Press, 1927. Pp. xv + 195.

3. *New Testament Word Studies*, by Ernest DeWitt Burton. Chicago : University of Chicago Press, 1927. Pp. xvi + 118.

4. *Education in a Democratic World*, by Ernest DeWitt Burton. Chicago : University of Chicago Press, 1927. Pp. xix + 165.

5. *Environmental Factors in Christian History*. With John T. McNeill and Matthew Spinka. Chicago : University of Chicago Press, 1939. Pp. x + 417.

6. *The Study of the Bible Today and Tomorrow*. Chicago : University of Chicago Press, 1947. Pp. xix + 436.

CONTRIBUTIONS TO BOOKS

1. "The New Birth Experience in Pauline Christianity and Contemporary Religions : A Genetic Study of Pauline Mysticism." *The University of Chicago Abstracts of Theses, Humanistic Series*, II, 453-60. Chicago : University of Chicago Press, 1926.

2. "The Study of Early Christianity." *Religious Thought in the Last Quarter Century*, ed. by Gerald B. Smith, pp. 42-69. Chicago: University of Chicago Press, 1927.

3. "Karahissar Ornament," "Evangelist Portraiture," and "The Leningrad Text Tableaux." *The Four Gospels of Karahissar*, Vol. I. *History and Text*, by Ernest Cadman Colwell, pp. 121-139. Chicago : University of Chicago Press, 1936.

4. "Current Contributions from Archaeology to Early Christian History." *Environmental Factors in Christian History*, Ed. by John T. McNeill, Matthew Spinka, and H. R. Willoughby, pp. 91-113. Chicago : University of Chicago Press, 1939.

5. "The Iconography of Cover Stamps and of Miniatures." *The Elizabeth Day McCormick Apocalypse*, Vol. II, *History and Text*, by Ernest Cadman Colwell, Ch. VIII (pp. 128-51). Chicago : University of Chicago Press, 1940.

6. "Archaic Crucifixion Iconography." *Munera Studiosa*, ed. by M. H. Shepherd, Jr. and S. E. Johnson, pp. 123-44. Cambridge : Episcopal Theological School, 1946.

7. "Mystery Initiation." *Contemporary Thinking about Paul*, compiled by Thomas S. Kepler, pp. 34-41. New York : Abingdon-Cokesbury Press, 1950.

ARTICLES

1. "The Next Step in New Testament Study," *JR*, II (1922), 159-78.

2. "The Study of Early Christianity during the Last Quarter Century," *JR*, VI (1926), 259-283.

3. "President Burton as his Unpublished Manuscripts Reveal Him," *UCM*, XIX (1927), 359-361.

4. "The Rockefeller-McCormick Manuscript," *The University Record*, XIV (1928), 153-157 (reprinted in "Magazine of the Art World," *Chicago Evening Post*, October 9, 1928).

5. "New Manuscript Acquisitions for Chicago : The Rockefeller-McCormick Testament," *UCM*, XXI (1929), 128-133.

6. "A Masterpiece of Byzantine Book Making," *Press Impressions*, VI (1929), 1-6.

7. "The Rockefeller-McCormick Manuscript and a Paleologan Cognate," *AJA*, XXXIV (1930), 48.

8. "A Year of Manuscript Acquisitions," *The University Record*, XVI (1930), 139-146.

9. "Manuscript Hunting in Chicago," *UCM*, XXIII (1930), 65-68.

10. "A Paleologan Family of Miniatured Manuscripts," *Parnassus*, III (1931), 45.

11. "The Vienna Genesis and the Rockefeller McCormick New Testament," *Art & Archeology*, XXXIII (1932), 275 (reprinted in *Art News*, Vol. 30, No. 34 (May 21, 1932), p. 14).

12. "The Reconstruction of Lost Rockefeller-McCormick Miniatures," *JBL*, LI (1932), 179-188.

13. "Lost Miniatures of the Rockefeller-McCormick Manuscript," *AJA*, XXXVI (1932), 39f.

14. "Codex 2400 and its Miniatures," *Art Bulletin*, XV (1933), 1-100.

15. "The Elizabeth Day McCormick Apocalypse : III. The Cycle of Text Illustrations," *JBL* LII (1933), 89-107.

16. "Current Errors Concerning the Coverdale Bible," *JBL*, LV (March 1936), 1-16.

17. "Decisive Data on Thomas Matthew Problems" (with Harold H. Hutson), *JBR*, VI (1938), 77-82, 121-128.

18. "A Unique Miniatured Greek Apocalypse," *Byzantion*, XIV (1939), 155-178.

19. "The Ignored Taverner Bible of 1539" (with Harold H. Hutson), *The Crozer Quarterly*, XVI (1939), 161-76.

20. "The Symbolism of Joseph Bond Chapel," *DSN*, VI (1939), 1-6.

21. "Fresh Archaeological Data concerning Christian Beginnings," *BA*, II (1939), 25-36.

22. "A Biographical Note," *Environmental Factors in Christian History*, ed. by McNeill, Spinka and Willoughby (Chicago : University of Chicago Press, 1939), pp. ix f.

23. "Greek Rebinding Colophons in Chicago Manuscripts," *Annales de l'Institut Kondakov* (Seminarium Kondakovianum), XI (1940), 21-32.

24. "Vagrant Folios from Family 2400 in the Free Library of Philadelphia," *Byzantion* (American Series, I), XV (1940-41), 126-132.

25. "Stray New Testament-Psalter Leaves Identified," *JBL*, LXI (1942), 57-60.

26. "Hans Holbein the Younger and the Coverdale Title Pages of 1535 and 1539-41," *ATR*, XXIV (1942), 106-118.

27. "Ethiopia," *Art of the United Nations* (Chicago : The Art Institute of Chicago, 1944), p. 24.

28. "Herbert Lockwood Willett," *Disciples Divinity House News*, XV (1944), 1 f.

29. "Bible, English," *Dictionary of Theology*, ed. by Vergilius Ferm (New York : Philosophical Library, 1945), pp. 70 f.

30. "Introduction," *The Study of the Bible Today and Tomorrow*, ed. by Harold R. Willoughby (Chicago : University of Chicago Press, 1947), pp. ix-xvi.

31. "Shirley Jackson Case, 1872-1947," *DSN*, XV (1948), 4 f.

32. "Shirley Jackson Case, 1872-1947," *UCM*, 40 (1948), 12 f.

33. "Goodspeed Week, October 15-23, 1948," *UCM*, 41 (1948), 1 f.

34. "Introduction," *The Bibliography and Biography of Shirley Jackson Case*, by Louis B. Jennings (Chicago : University of Chicago Press, 1949), pp. v f.

35. "To You, Mr. Chips," *Tilton School Bulletin*, XL (1950), 8 f.

36. "To William Andrew Irwin," *DSN*, XVII (1950), 8-10.

37. "Representational Biblical Cycles : Antiochian and Constantinopolitan," *JBL*, LXIX (1950), 129-36.

38. "The Distinctive Sources of Palestinian Pilgrimage Iconography," *JBL*, LXXIV (1955), 61-68.

39. "The Bibliography of Amos Niven Wilder," *Harvard Divinity School Bulletin*, 21 (1955-56), 151-59.

40. "The Religious Import of the Tushingham Plaque," *Vigiliae Christianae*, XI (1957), 57-92.

41. "The Acceptance of the 1958 Gutenberg Award for Edgar Johnson Goodspeed," *DSN*, XXV (1958), 18-23.

42. "Rist of Iliff and Hough of Drew : Co-Interpreters to John of Patmos," *The Iliff Review*, XV (1958), 29-43.

43. Two major articles acceipted for publication in *The Interpreter's Dictionary of the Bible*, ed. by George A. Buttrick.

44. Twelve minor articles accepted for publication in *Hasting's Dictionary of the Bible* (Revised One-Volume Edition), ed. by F. C. Grant and H. H. Rowley.

BOOK REVIEWS

1. T. R. Glover : *Paul of Tarsus* and W. L. Knox : *St. Paul and the Church of Jerusalem*, *JR*, VI (1926), 98-101.

2. F. J. Foakes-Jackson : *The Life of Saint Paul*, *JR*, VII (1927), 98-101.

3. A. E. J. Rawlinson: *The New Testament Doctrine of the Christ*, CC, XLIV (1927), 145.

4. T. W. Goodspeed : *Ernest De Witt Burton; A Biographical Sketch*, *UCM*, XX (1927), 40-42.

5. F. J. Foakes-Jackson : *Peter, Prince of Apostles*, CC, XLIV (1927), 1457.

6. F. J. Foakes-Jackson : *Peter, Prince of Apostles*, *JR*, VIII (1928), 136-38.

7. Thomas Wilson : *St. Paul and Paganism*, *JR*, IX (1929), 132-34.

8. C. C. McCown : *The Genesis of the Social Gospel*, *Religious Education*, XXV (1930), 82 f.

9. J. W. Jack : *Samaria in Ahab's Time*, *Religious Education*, XXV (1930), 85.

10. W. A. Heidel : *The Day of Jahweh*, CP, XXV (1930), 84-86.

11. E. F. Scott: *The Gospel and its Tributaries*, *JR*, X (1930), 271-63.

12. Arthur Holmes : *The Mind of Paul*, *JR*, X (1930), 597-600.

13. W. K. Lowther-Clark: *New Testament Problems*, *JR*, XI (1931), 120-22.

14. F. C. Porter : *The Mind of Christ in Paul*, *Religious Education*, XXVI (1931), 371 f.

15. R. P. de Jerphanion : *La Voix des Monuments*, *JR*, XI (1931), 616-19.

16. R. P. Casey : *Serapion of Thmuis, Against the Manichees*, CH, I (1932), 173 f.

17. E. F. Scott : *The Literature of the New Testament*, CC, XLIX (1932), 1274.

18. Elwood Worcester : *Studies in the Birth of Our Lord*, CH, II (1933), 110 f.

19. G. H. Box : *Early Christianity and its Rivals*, *JR*, XIII (1933), 330.

20. N. Levison : *The Jewish Background of Christianity*, *JR*, XIII (1933), 331.

21. A. D. Nock : *Conversion*, *JR*, XIV (1934), 377 f.

22. Erwin R. Goodenough : *By Light, Light; The Mystic Gospel of Hellenistic Judaism*, *ATR*, XVII (1935), 36-38.

23. William Fairweather, *The Background of the Epistles*, *JR*, XVI (1936), 112.

24. W. H. P. Hatch: *The Greek Manuscripts of the New Testament in Jerusalem*, *JR*, XVI (1936), 113.

25. W. H. P. Hatch: *The Greek Manuscripts of the New Testament at Mount Sinai*, *JR*, XVI (1936), 113.

26. Benedikt Kraft: *Die Handschriften der Bisch. Ordinariats-bibliothek in Augsburg*, *JR*, XVI (1936), 115.

27. W. O. E. Oesterley: *An Introduction to the Books of the Apococrypha*, *JR*, XVI (1936), 119 f.

28. V. C. C. Collum: *The Tressé Iron Age Megalithic Monument*, *JR*, XVI (1936), 203-205.

29. A. E. Bailey: *Christ in Recent Art*, *JR*, XVI (1936), 237.

30. J. F. Mozley: *William Tyndale*, *JR*, XVIII (1938), 243 f.

31. Erwin R. Goodenough: *Religious Myth and Tradition*, *JR*, XVIII (1938), 366.

32. M. O. Percival: *William Blake's Circle of Destiny*. *JR*, XVIII (1938), 370.

33. Casey, Lake and Lake: *Quantulacumque; Studies Presented to Kirsopp Lake by Pupils, Colleagues, and Friends*, *JBL*, LVII (1938), 353 f.

34. C. J. Cadoux: *Ancient Smyrna*, *JR*, XIX (1939), 84 f.

35. Erwin R. Goodenough: *The Politics of Philo Judaeus; Practice and Theory*, *JR*, XIX (1939), 183 f.

36. Meyer Waxman: *A History of Jewish Literature*, *JR*, XIX (1939) 415f.

37. Solomon Zeitlin: *The Book of Jubilees; Its Character and Significance*, *JR*, XX (1940), 324.

38. Samuel Belkin: *Philo and the Oral Law*, *JR*, XX (1940), 408.

39. Charles Guignebert: *The Jewish World in the Time of Jesus*, *JR*, XX (1940), 101.

40. Erwin R. Goodenough: *An Introduction to Philo Judaeus*, *JR*, XXI (1941), 103.

41. M. P. Nilsson: *Greek Popular Religion*, *JR*, XXI (1941), 230.

42. Campbell Bonner: *The Homily on the Passion by Melito, Bishop of Sardis*, *CH*, X (1941), 74 f.

43. William G. Braude: *Jewish Proselyting in the First Three Centuries of the Common Era*, *JR*, XXI (1941), 227 f.

44. Emerson Swift: *Hagia Sophia*, *JR*, XXI (1941), 470-72.

45. Hermann Vogelstein: *History of Jews in Rome*, *JR*, XXII (1942), 231 f.

46. C.-M. Edsman: *Le baptême de feu*, *JBL*, LXI (1942), 68 f.

47. C. C. Butterworth: *The Literary Lineage of the King James Bible*, *JR*, XXII (1942), 331 f.

48. P. S. Minear: *And Great Shall be Your Reward*, *JR*, XXII (1942), 227.

49. S. M. Crosby: *The Abbey of St. Denis, 475-1122*, *CH*, XI (1942), 332-34.

50. Solomon Zeitlin: *Who Crucified Jesus?*, *CC*, LX (1943), 109-10.

51. C. R. Morey: *Mediaeval Art, New Testament Literature in 1942* (Chicago, 1943), p. 4.

52. C. C. McCown: *The Ladder of Progress in Palestine, Bulletin of Pacific School of Religion*, XXII (1943), 6.

53. Terenzig Poladian: *A Collection of Prayers from the Ancient Armenian Book of Divine Liturgy, JR*, XXIV (1944), 303.

54. F. C. Grant: *The Earliest Gospel, CC*, LXI (1944), 275 f.

55. Leo Auerbach: *The Babylonian Talmud in Selection, JR*, XXV (1945) 70.

56. A. E. Bailey: *The Arts and Religion, CTSR*, XXXV (1945), 36.

57. Hans Swarzenski: *The Berthold Missal and the Scriptorium of the Weingarten Abbey, Speculum*, XX (1945), 125 f.

58. R. G. Anderson: *The Biography of a Cathedral, CH*, XIV (1945), 131 f.

59. Paul Friedländer: Documents of Dying Paganism, *CP*, XL (1945) 263 f.

60. Jack Finegan: *Light from the Ancient Past: The Archeological Background of the Hebrew-Christian Religion, American Historical Review*, LI (1946), 700-702.

61. Ernest Wright and Floyd Filson: *The Westminster Historical Atlas of the Bible, JR*, XXVI (1946), 138 f.

62. George Elderkin: *Archaeological Papers VIII, Golgotha, Kraneion, and the Holy Sepulcher, JR*, XXVI (1946), 152.

63. Lake and Lake: *Dated Greek Minuscule Manuscripts to the Year 1200, CP*, XLI (1946), 249.

64. C. C. Torrey: *The Apocryphal Literature; A Brief Introduction, JNES*, V (1946), 280 f.

65. Franz Landsberger: *A History of Jewish Art, JBL*, LXVI (1947), 249-251.

66. W. W. Hyde: *Paganism to Christianity in the Roman Empire, JBL*, LXVI (1947), 351-53.

67. W. F. Volbach: *Early Christian Mosaics, JR*, XXVII (1947), 225.

68. C. P. Maus: *The World's Great Madonnas, Crozer Quarterly*, XXV (1948), 72 f.

69. Creaghan and Raubitschek: *Early Christian Epitaphs from Athens, CP*, XLIII (1948), 272 f.

70. Walter Lowrie: *Art in the Early Church, Christendom*, XIII (1948), 260 f.

71. E. L. Sukenik: *The Earliest Records of Christianity, JBL*, LXVIII (1949), 61-65.

72. Otto von Simson: *Sacred Fortress: Byzantine Art in Ravenna, CH*, XVIII (1949), 55 f.

73. Ian Fraser: *Understanding the New Testament, CTSR*, XXXIX (1949), 37 f.

74. Robert Pfeiffer: *History of New Testament Times with an Introduction to the Apocrypha, JNES*, IX (1950), 117 f.

75. Willard Sperry: *Jesus Then and Now, Crozer Quarterly*, XXVII (1950), 54 f.

76. Parvis and Wikgren : *New Testament Manuscript Studies*, *JR*, XXX (1950), 276 f.

77. Willem den Boer: *Scriptorum paganorum I-IV saec. de Christianis testimonia*, *CP*, XLVI (1951), 133.

78. Saul Liebermann : *Hellenism in Jewish Palestine*, *Crozer Quarterly*, XXVII (1951), 272-74.

79. S. V. McCasland : *By the Finger of God: Demon Possession and Exorcism in Early Christianity*, *CH*, XX (1951), 91-93.

80. Moses Hadas : *Aristeas to Philocrates*, *CTSR*, XLI (1951), 33.

81. Floyd Filson : *The New Testament Against its Environment*, *CTSR*, XLI (1951), 33.

82. Samson Eitrem : *Some Notes on Demonology in the New Testament*, *CP*, XLVII (1952), 256 f.

83. Ralph Stob : *Christianity and Classical Civilization*, *CP*, XLVII (1952), 257-59.

84. S. E. Johnson (ed.) : *The Joy of Study: Papers on New Testament Presented to Honor Frederick Clifton Grant*, *JBL*, LXXI (1952), 185-87.

85. W. H. P. Hatch : *Facsimiles and Descriptions of Minuscule Manuscripts of the New Testament*, *Speculum*, XXVII (1952), 387-90.

86. S. Davis : *Race Relations in Ancient Egypt*, *JR*, XXXIII (1953), 65 f.

87. E. F. Scott : *The Crisis in the Life of Jesus*, *CTSR*, XLIII (1953), 43 f.

88. Robert M. Grant : *Miracle and Natural Law in Graeco-Roman and Early Christian Thought*, *CP*, XLVIII (1953), 269-71.

89. J. R. Coates : *Bible Key Words from Gerhard Kittel's Theologisches Wörterbuch zum Neuen Testament*, *CTSR*, XLIII (1953), 34.

90. J. G. Davies : *The Origin and Development of Early Christian Church Architecture*, *Religion in Life*, XXII (1953), 473-75.

91. E. J. Goodspeed : *As I Remember*, *JBR*, XXII (1954), 44 f.

92. Moses Hadas : *The Third and Fourth Books of Maccabees*, *CTSR*, XLIV (1954), 34.

93. F. C. Grant: *Hellenistic Religions: The Age of Syncretism*, *JBL*, LXXIII (1954), 171 f.

94. E. A. Rumball-Petre : *Rare Bibles: An Introduction for Collectors and a Descriptive Checklist*, *CC*, LXXI (1954), 926-27.

95. A. J. Festugière : *Personal Religion Among the Greeks*, *CP*, L (1955), 290-92.

96. Anton Fridrichsen : *The Root of the Vine: Essays in Biblical Theology*, *CTSR*, XLV (1955), 29.

97. Erwin R. Goodenough : *Jewish Symbols in the Graeco-Roman Period*, Vols. I-IV, *Archeological Evidence and Methodology*, *JNES*, XV (1956), 121-23.

98. N. W. DeWitt : *St. Paul and Epicurus*, *CP*, LI, (1956), 124-27.

99. John Knox : *The Early Church and the Coming Great Church*, *JBL*, LXXV (1956), 240 f.

100. Ethelbert Stauffer : *Christ and the Caesars: Historical Sketches*, *JR*, XXXVI (1956), 265 f.

101. Samuel Sandmel : *A Jewish Understanding of the New Testament*, *JNES*, XVI (1957), 273-75.

102. S. M. Gilmore : *The Gospel Jesus Preached, CTSR,* XLVIII (1958), 20 f.

103. Erwin R. Goodenough : *Jewish Symbols in the Graeco-Roman Period, Vols. V and VI, Fish, Bread, and Wine, JNES,* XVII (1958), 58-60.

104. Bruce Metzger : *Introduction to the Apocrypha, Revised Standard Version, JNES,* XVIII (1959), 100-102.

105. Carl H. Kraeling: *The Synagogue* ("The Excavations at Dura-Europos," Final Report VIII, Part 1), *JNES,* XX (1961), 52-57.

106. Reviews of the following volumes are shortly to be printed in the *Journal of Near Eastern Studies:*

Arnold J. Toynbee: *Hellenism: The History of a Civilization.*

Erwin R. Goodenough : *Jewish Symbols in the Graeco-Roman Period, Vols. VII and VIII, Pagan Symbols in Judaism.*

ABBREVIATIONS

Names of periodicals are usually spelled out in their first occurrence. Where more than one citation occurs, and in the case of a few other works, the following abbreviations may be used.

AJA	*American Journal of Archeology*
ATR	*Anglican Theological Review*
BA	*Biblical Archaeologist*
BASOR	*Bulletin of the American Schools of Oriental Research*
CC	*Christian Century*
CH	*Church History*
CP	*Classical Philology*
CTSR	*Chicago Theological Seminary Register*
DSN	*Divinity School News*
HE	*Historia Ecclesiastica*
ICC	*International Critical Commentary*
JBL	*Journal of Biblical Literature and Exegesis*
JBR	*Journal of Bible and Religion*
JNES	*Journal of Near Eastern Studies*
JR	*Journal of Religion*
JTS	*Journal of Theological Studies*
Judaism	George Foote Moore, *Judaism in the First Centuries of the Christian Era: The Age of the Tannaim*, 3 vols. (Cambridge, Mass., 1927, 1930)
NTS	*New Testament Studies*
P-W	Pauly-Wissowa-Kroll, *Realenzyclopädie der klassischen Altertumswissenschaft* (Stuttgart, 1893 ff.)
Texte u. Unters.	*Texte und Untersuchungen zur Geschichte der altchristlichen Literatur*
UCM	*The University of Chicago Magazine*
ZNW	*Zeitschrift für die neutestamentliche Wissenschaft*